BUDDHA
BREAKING UP

A GUIDE TO HEALING FROM HEARTACHE
& LIBERATING YOUR AWESOMENESS

STEPHANEE KILLEN

Published by Parham Press
www.parhampress.com

ISBN: 978-0-9889105-0-8

Second Edition
Printed in the United States of America

Names have been changed in order to preserve the anonymity of the parties involved.

Visit the author at www.buddhabreakingup.com
or on Facebook at www.facebook.com/BuddhaBreakingUp

Parham Press

CONTENTS

Author's Note Regarding Gender-Specific Pronouns

I have chosen to address the reader using primarily feminine pronouns; therefore, when I refer to a relationship partner, it may be in the form of "him," "boyfriend," "husband," or "ex-partner." This is to minimize the amount of awkwardness that can occur when trying to refer to both genders equally; however, please note that while women are statistically more likely to pick up a book on dealing with a breakup, this book is equally relevant for men. In fact, the principle message of this work is also relevant for those of us who may be struggling with relationships in general—not just the loss of one but also the ongoing maintenance of those in which we are still engaged. While the focus of this book deals with a break from our primary romantic relationship partner, the methods described for moving on may be beneficial for coming to terms with any dramatic change that creates a distinct and powerful feeling of loss, sorrow, anger, or groundlessness.

"The wound is the place where the light enters you..."

—Rumi

MOST BOOKS ABOUT breakups seem to start with a story telling you about a breakup. That sounds reasonable but tedious. *I* don't even want to hear *that* story. Then again, I lived it. Besides, it really just went like this:

A. Woman meets Man.
B. Woman falls madly in love with Man.
C. Man deeply appreciates that Woman falls madly in love. *("Aw, shucks, kitten.")*
D. They give it a go *(for four years)*.
E. Woman eventually realizes that Step **"B"** actually sucks without a little **"M"** *(for Mutuality)*.
F. Woman and Man break up.
G. Woman is devastated. *(She secretly hopes that Step **"F"** will lead to the reciprocation of **"B"** so that they can get to the **"M"** [for Mutuality and Marriage.])*
H. Man abruptly gets back together with ex. *(Wtf?!)*
I. Woman is left alone to re-discover **"I."**

There. That should suffice, right? I'm sure this story sounds familiar. Of course, it's missing the particulars, but the gist of it is enough. We each have our own personal history and baggage we carry with us, which flavors the story and makes it uniquely our own. Heartbreak, however, is not unique. It is universal. It is the great equalizer. Loss can bring us to our knees, no matter whether those knees are inside a pair of $250,000 Dussault Apparel's Trashed Denim jeans or $18 Faded Glories from Wal-Mart. This story is ancient. Would it make any difference to tell you that I first met James in high school? That I'd loved him even then, but the timing was wrong? Meeting him fifteen years later seemed like fate. Upon seeing him again (at a Blues benefit where he was sitting in on bass), I knew he was *The One.* Our email and telephone exchanges while he was on tour (and well after his return) convinced me that no one could understand him the way I could. No one could see his shadow side *and love him for it* the way I could. I would marry this man. *I was the woman for him.*

I was also entirely and completely wrong on that count. Turns out, I was *not* the woman for him—at least for any significant length of time. Our story was going to be considerably shorter than the lifetime together I'd imagined. The details don't matter as much as the feelings that came after.

That's the story I'm going to tell.

What happens when you are shattered? What happens when all you can think to yourself is, THIS ISN'T FAIR AND LIFE IS CRUEL? What happens when you feel so low you begin to believe you can't take another step forward? Maybe you don't *want* to take another step forward. This is hard stuff. This is the stuff that drives us to the very edge of annihilation. At least it feels that way. It feels like a very real obliteration of the self.

Let me tell you this: *It feels that way because it is.*

This breakdown can be the worst thing that's ever happened to you, or it can be the best thing for precisely this moment in your life. Hey, I'm not telling you this while looking down from some lofty height where I have magically met my soulmate, am happily married, and can easily say, "Well, thank goodness that ended so life could bring me the man I was *supposed* to be with." Nor am I going to be approaching you from a place of resigned spinsterhood and bitterness. *Get thee to a nunnery. Relationships are the root of all evil.* This isn't the case. I hope to find love again. Rarely a day goes by when I don't wish for intimate companionship—at least it's not every *moment* of every day, but still, companionship would be nice.

The truth is that I had a choice. It's the same choice you have right now. There is that moment when the break occurs, and we are faced with the complete destruction of everything we thought we knew—not just about our beloved partner but also about ourselves. It feels as if our very identity has been stolen. We are no longer quite sure who we are in this new context. We are no longer certain what our path is meant to be. Worse, we feel more vulnerable than we've ever felt. If the relationship ended before we were ready for it to end, then the chances are good that we feel *lessened*—as if something precious were stolen from us—and it can be difficult to feel anything at all positive in this experience. All we have are grief and loss.

Only…technically, no one has died. For those grieving what is considered a *real* loss—death—the bereaved are often provided with the basic benefit of society's understanding, if not their acceptance that this grief is a *significant* process. You can take time off of work if a loved one dies, but if you stay home too many days because you just broke up with your boyfriend or divorced your partner, not only will everyone look at you like you're crazy, but you're also very likely to get fired. Your friends get tired of hearing you talk about your pain and wonder when you'll be getting over it. Your family becomes exasperated when you keep rehashing the same hurt feelings over and over again. Normally, there are others who will share in the grieving process with you when someone dies; but when a relationship dies, you're left to grieve the loss alone. And while the unbearable truth is that, in a physical death, you know you will never see that person again, in the death of a relationship, you live in a twofold fear: that you will suddenly encounter your ex-partner *and* that you will never see him again *even though he is still alive!* From day to day, you are never quite sure which would be worse.

So, how in the world can this complete destruction be the best thing that ever happened to you?

I'm glad you asked….

How is this possibly the best thing for precisely this moment in my life?

One word: Evolution.

Okay, it's a lofty word. It's probably the last word you want to hear right now in the midst of your heartbreak. But moments when we are completely broken like this, at our most vulnerable, are also the moments when the universe is providing us with the best opportunity to review some very important elemental rules. You'll notice the essence of these rules resurfacing in various real-life circumstances throughout the course of this book. Dealing with these facts of life is a necessary part of the process. It's okay if they don't all make sense to you right now—or if you find yourself feeling resistant to them—especially if your loss is new. In time, you may come to embrace them.

RULE #1: WALLS DON'T REALLY PROTECT YOU

As much as you may feel like walling yourself off from other people right now, this strategy typically only serves to further enhance your feelings of sorrow. Living as a Closed System means that nothing new can come into whatever circle you have drawn for yourself. The air is recycled. So is your pain. Closing ourselves off to others is part of the reason there is so much suffering in the world. Not only does this behavior limit our evolutionary potential but it also stunts our growth on an emotional level.

Living as an Open System may invite pain, but it also invites pleasure. By being an Open System, we can admit and integrate new things. This integration of new things (new ideas, new concepts, new events, new ways of doing things) increases the richness of our lives. We create greater depth, including a greater depth of character.

RULE #2: GROWTH FREQUENTLY OCCURS FROM A BREAKDOWN

We often perceive growth as a painful process, and this pain tends to be the result of something breaking down. When we exercise a muscle and feel the strain the next day, this is because in order to grow that muscle, we must first tear and repair the fibers. When we plant a seed, in order for the plant to develop, it must first press against the seed lining, splitting it apart in the process of emerging.

As we increase the richness and depth of our lives, we may find that other things begin to break down from the force of that growth. Indeed, your relationship may have fallen prey to this very force. Of course, now that breakdown has left you in a very painful place, but this place also serves as fertile soil for that growth. Sometimes, the more complex something becomes, the more likely it is either to experience a massive evolutionary leap (think here in terms of paradigm shifts, or suddenly experiencing a significant insight that changes the way you view yourself and the world) or a complete breakdown. The good news is that regardless of which one of these occurs, both may serve an equal purpose!

A dissipative structure (an object with a continuous flow of energy passing through it, such as human beings!) can use that energy to reorganize in ways that create a higher level of functioning. This means that even if something breaks down, *it can still reorganize in ways that are superior to its original form.* As long as we remain open, we always have the opportunity to change and evolve.

Everything in nature points to the fact that life is ever-changing. Energy never dies. The famous Sufi poet Rumi said, "Don't grieve. Anything you lose comes round in another form." What if we quit struggling against a natural process that requires openness to change, since change is going to take place whether we like it or not? In fact, the very instability we experience in life provides us with amazing opportunities to evolve, to reform ourselves, to become something new *and* better. We can become more sophisticated, more INTEGRATED. A lack of change, a lack of movement, often leads to STAGNATION.

Rule #3: Learn to Create and Then Let Go

Something that we have worked very hard to build has just broken down. Now we are in pain. It feels miserable. It is very difficult to let go of what we worked so hard to create, especially our *vision* of that thing—what we imagined it could be regardless of what was actually there. (In most cases, it's the vision of what we wanted that we cling to the longest, since as rational beings, we know that the actuality of what may have been right there in front of us was long overdue for demolition.) Regardless, chances are good that we invested a lot of time and energy into what we were trying to create, and now we are left asking ourselves, "What was the point of that?" It seems like it was all for nothing. What we *really* wanted to get out of it was happiness, love, and peace. Maybe we believed these things would come in the form of a lasting marriage—a real union and partnership so that we could feel supported in our lives. Now that it's over, we ask, "What happens next?"

Now we must turn our energy toward creating a change in perspective. It is unlikely that we'll stop thinking in terms of good or bad overnight. It's going to be pretty difficult *not* to see this as a bad thing, and it's this thinking that is going to cause us a lot of pain in the days ahead. We will go back through every moment of our past relationship. We will second-guess everything we ever said or did. We will wonder whether we could have done more, said more, *changed* more. And the answer? The answer doesn't matter. It doesn't matter because we can't move backwards. That means that the best we can do right now is to change our perspective regarding what is good and what is bad. When we insist upon clinging to a particular perspective, or person for that matter, we become more of a Closed System. We shut down. New things (or people) cannot enter. We begin to forget all about the other sides of the equation we chose not to explore when we decided to settle down with our recently ex-significant other in the first place.

Naturally, when things break down, as all things do (even if not through a breakup, we will suffer other losses), we get lost in the pieces—we get lost in trying to reshape them *into something familiar*. We want to put them back into a recognizable framework so that we can get to work again building that thing we've held so dearly in our minds. Wanting to create is not the problem. Wanting a framework for our lives is not the problem. It's attachment to the pieces of that old frame that is the problem.

That means we have to learn to let go. The truth is that no matter how connected we feel to and with another person, we possess nothing. Not really. Even when we have a grand, mutual love, we must still contend with death. No one physical form is eternal. Love may be enduring but perhaps not the physical forms we use to contain or identify that love.

When love is *not* enduring, when something is clearly shaking us off, our task is to let go. That's it. Just let go. That's the part, of course, that is much easier said than done. But without this ability to let go, we limit our growth. We also limit what we are able to take in and create next.

RULE #4: LIFE IS NOT STATIC

We are far less fixed and unyielding than we think. Most of the cells in our bodies renew themselves on average of every ten to fifteen years. Our red blood cells last only an average of 120 days. The surface layer of our skin is recycled every two weeks. Our liver cells renew in six weeks. Our very bones are in the process of dissolving and rebuilding every ten years.[1]

Eventually this process may slow as we age, but suffice to say that at this moment, even the body that you used to share with your ex-partner is in the process of renewing itself. We are changing and ever-*exchanging*. The notion that we are beings firmly set in our bodies and ways, far apart from each other, is illusion. The notion that we can't let go is also illusion. The only thing that seems static is our MIND—our MEMORIES, the way we choose to process information. Your body, your bones, your very cells are already moving on. It's your mind that has to catch up.

RULE #5: LIFE IS A CYCLE THAT INCLUDES DISSOLUTION

The engine of life is a cycle that includes Creation, Maintenance, Evolution, and Dissolution.

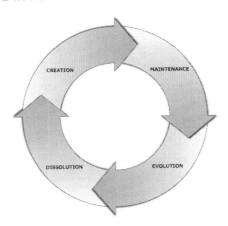

Sometimes, we get our limbs tangled in the mechanics of this cycle trying to get it to stop spinning, and then it feels like we might lose an arm. My advice? Stop putting your arm in there!

Right now, you are in the Dissolution stage.

In the practice of Shaivism, Shaivites believe that Lord Shiva, rather than being the God of destruction, actually performs five actions—creation, preservation, dissolution, concealing grace, and revealing grace. Each of these actions corresponds to a name and form of Shiva. Creation is associated with Sadyojata (akin to Brahma); Preservation, with Vamadeva (akin to Vishnu); and Dissolution, with Aghora (akin to Rudra). These are all forms taken by Shiva. As Brahma, Shiva creates. As Vishnu, Shiva preserves. As Rudra/Aghora, he dissolves. These actions are all important aspects of the *same* cycle, not something that should be considered separately and categorized as good or evil, as in the concept that creation must come from God alone, so then destruction must only come from the devil.[2]

The experience of dissolution is very painful, but it is also a very necessary aspect of life's cycle. Revealing Grace is a part of this process, and I firmly believe that it's our vulnerability, the opening that arises when we have been cracked apart and we find ourselves groundless, which reveals to us the true grace of life—if we let it. There is beauty even in our grieving. We have an opportunity here to truly feel what is going on around us—to see the face of our neighbor and know that his or her heart aches as well; to feel the woundedness in others, even those whom we feel have done us wrong. This is the chance we have to open our eyes to what is going on around us. As we move through our grief, and life beings to spin again into creation, the hope is that we take this new grace with us. We integrate these lessons into our spirits and actions and the ways that we approach our relationships in the future. This isn't baggage that we cart around, battered and ugly… it isn't something we shove into the closet and hope that it doesn't pop out at an inopportune time. This is an event that can make us *more* beautiful, more open, more capable of love than we were before.

This means that, at some point, once you're through the worst of the breaking apart, you can be thankful that it happened in the first place.

So, thank you, to the man who broke my heart.
Inside it was another one, and I am growing it to be bigger.

Hold on.

Before the whole " 'nother one and growing it to be bigger" bit, there was the bit where the first one caught fire and fried itself most spectacularly down into ash. I rolled around in that ash. There was much pulling of hair and gnashing of teeth. There was also a lot of dripping of nose and swelling of eyes. It wasn't pretty. Honestly, right after the breakup, I thought, *Yes. I can do this. This will be okay.* I even got the bright idea to blog about it. You know…because certainly other people could benefit from the total disaster that had literally *just* taken place in my life, right?

This strained optimism (and ability to be generally coherent and upright) lasted precisely seven days.

We'll start there—back when I thought I could handle everything just fine.

PART I
THE STORY OF U̶S̶ ME

Oct. 5, 2011

Break up; as in to separate or be separated into pieces. Break down; as in, to cause to collapse; destroy. Break out; as in, to emerge or escape; to isolate. Break through; as in, to make a sudden, quick advance.

MY BRAIN GOT me into this. It's entirely responsible. (My brain begs to differ. It says my heart got me into this, and now it's left cleaning up the mess.) It made a decision—one that was most definitely not in agreement with my heart—and now my brain has left me in the lurch. (*"Consequences, baby,"* it says, not sounding the least bit remorseful.) But I say, if it's going to make choices like these, shouldn't it also turn off the pain receptors? You know, those ones making it feel as if someone is stabbing me, repeatedly, in the chest?

No. Evidently, there is no reprieve. I'm never more reminded of how difficult it is, engaging in this *human being,* when I'm forced to face the very human tendency to grasp. Ask me to stop grasping; just see what happens. Letting go has never been my strong suit. That's putting it lightly. Let me rephrase: Letting go is something I JUST DON'T DO. I can't. My hands are completely incapable of opening themselves to let something go. Give me a handful of thorns and you'd better believe I'm going to hold onto it. I mean, I have it, don't I? And if I let it go, what will I have then? Bloody palms with nothing to show for it, that's what.

Mostly I don't let go because I've convinced myself there's a good reason why I'm holding on. In this case, it wasn't a *thing* I was holding onto. It was a person. And my good reason was noble: love. THE Love. You know? The one you tell yourself is THE ONE. (And then you tell yourself that THE ONE means the one you will marry and be with for eternity instead of simply THE ONE who tells it to you like it is, rips out your heart so you can examine it a little more closely, and then walks off as if this is all perfectly reasonable.) It turns out though, that since by now I *know* I'm a total failure at letting go, I owed it to the universe to do something about it. I got it into my head that the universe would be mightily displeased with me if, after all this time, I was still messing around with this business about grasping. So, I *am* capable of letting go, but the part where I feel equanimity? The part where I feel good about letting go? I'm not even close. I would like to say that at least I was *courageous...* But—

Courage only carries you so far. Shakespeare knew. "Courage man, the hurt cannot be much," says Romeo to Mercutio, after he's been stabbed. To which Mercutio responds, "...ask for me tomorrow, and you will find me a grave man." Mercutio knew. Courage does not stop you from dying.

I'm not dying. I'm in my mid-thirties, and I've finally learned this little ditty: Open hand. Release.

Let me tell you: It *feels* like dying.

Love doesn't know about all the fairy tale structures we try to build around it. It is completely unaware, for instance, that when I love someone, it is also supposed to mean that it *works out*. As in, I love them, they love me, and we both live so hap-pi-ly.

Love, right now, looks more like this . . .

I can't get words out without sobbing. It's unattractive. Under-statement. I am a gross caricature of myself. My eyes are red. I've cried off every single ounce of makeup. If it weren't for the tissue I am holding up to my nose, I would be leaking. Leaking everywhere. Eyes, nose, mouth. This hurricane force of grief is shaking my foundations. Added to that, my attempts to STOP myself from crying have caused a jagged log or some sort of boulder to lodge itself into my esophagus. Also, I can no longer breathe. My nasal passages have shrunk to the size of a Barbie doll's left nostril and then promptly filled with fluid. My head is being squeezed by a vice. I can barely move it without splinters of pain jabbing at my eyeballs.

My stomach is twisting. I have tried to eat food, but it appears to be impossible to actually swallow past the mountain jammed in my throat. Instead, I take an Advil, then sit in the bathroom with the shower on full hot and poke my head around the shower curtain to breathe it in. I need to breathe. I need to breathe. I need to
b r e a t h e.

Eventually, the griefquake subsides. It's a temporary reprieve. I know this well from past experience. It will last five minutes. It will last until I think about something. Anything. Until I look around and see the evidence of him everywhere. Trying to sleep is the next most difficult thing. What happens is that you fall asleep okay because you've cried yourself into exhaustion. Then, you wake up, suddenly, and everything comes flooding back. You have just lost the love of your life (**So far**, you tell yourself. *Please God let me have enough life left that it only be SO FAR*), and you are alone. The house is empty. It will remain empty. You squeeze your eyes shut and pray to God, any God will do—or even a saint. In my case, it was Saint Raphael. There is no patron saint of the brokenhearted, but they call Rafi the "Medicine of God." He is the patron saint of the blind and of travelers, so somehow I make it fit. I am blinded by grief and traveling toward the edge of a cliff.

"Just let me sleep," I beg him. "I will go with you where you want me to go; only please…let me breathe…sleep."

I wake, and the feeling is still there. Love. It's easier then, in the end, to remember the beginning. In the beginning, it's all running through a field of daisies, right? Even when you tell yourself it's not. If you're an adult with any kind of relationship experience under your belt, you sit yourself down and have a stern talk. You say, "Self." And self says, *"Yes."* You say, "There are no fairy tales. You know that, right? That gooey deliciousness you're feeling is normal. But reality will eventually set in. And no one is perfect. We all have our flaws and baggage and weathered bits." Self nods its head in enthusiastic agreement. *"I know, I know,"* that head nod says. "So no walking into this all shiny-eyed and ridiculous," you warn. And self shakes its head, all shiny-eyed and ridiculous. *"Roger that,"* the head shake says. *It'll be different this time,* is what it means.

But, Love, later? Love presiding over the Death of Relationship? Love when you know that Love and Relationship don't necessarily have to co-exist? That is a different picture. It is a messy picture—one that involves a lot of leaking, and swelling, and sleeplessness. It might also involve gallons of Dublin Mudslide Ben and Jerry's, with copious amounts of Shiraz poured on like hot fudge and little sprinkles of Valium bits.

But since I neither eat ice cream nor drink alcohol (and there isn't anything stronger than Advil and homeopathic cold remedies in my medicine cabinet), I am alarmingly lucid. Apparently, ginger tea does not have a numbing effect. I get the pleasure of fully experiencing this *experience.*

I weep at the slightest provocation. I sound fine one moment, and the next, I am weeping! I cannot go to my Facebook page. Facebook! What new form of relationship-ending torture is this social networking tenth circle of hell? Who is going to change the relationship status first? Should it be quick, like yanking out an arrow that's been jammed into your solar plexus, or slowly, later, after everyone (and by everyone, I mean just me) has calmed down and can look at a stupid Facebook relationship status without, you guessed it, bursting into tears. It's uncertain which is worse: seeing it there, or that moment when you don't. And what about co-mingled friends and family? What is the protocol? How can I politely de-friend everyone and explain that while I really like you quite a bit, thank you, and it was wonderful to know you, seeing any of your posts now sends me into paroxysms (yes, I said *paroxysms*) of tears. Probably not coincidentally, I found a white hair just a moment ago.

This love shit is for the birds. I assume it's like having a baby. While you're giving birth, you swear that you will never, EVER, ever have another. In fact, you swear off sex entirely. But you don't. And so, the same goes with this. This love shit is for the birds. Why go through it when this is what happens on the other end?

Thankfully, I have family and friends. They are the keepers of my heart. That broken thing, I hand to them. Somehow, they are able to look at this tattered remnant and catalogue a list of things that make it beautiful. They swear it will mend. They swear it will be all one piece again. I nod. But what I don't say is, *"You keep it. I'd just as soon not have that ridiculous thing thumping around in my chestal region, thank you very much."*

And so ends Day One.

DAY 2
PRAYERS TO THE WOODBLOCK FROG

IT'S DAY 2, and I want an Ashram. I want to chant *Ham-sa* over and over again, in India, like Elizabeth Gilbert in *Eat, Pray, Love*. I want to become a devotee of something. Myself, maybe. I will set up an altar in the living room, where I will kneel every day and pray to my little woodblock guiro frog: "Oh venerable frog," I might say, "in absence of some other physical representation of the divine, maybe *you* could help me figure out precisely what I should be praying for this time."

The frog probably won't say anything, but then, I wouldn't expect it to. It's crazy enough talking to a guiro frog without expecting it to actually *console* you.

This is in spite of the fact that, the previous night, my best friend Josh, from his lofty perch somewhere in the mountains of Colorado, tried to console me with the story of his rosebush again. It didn't stick. This morning, I woke up to the sun streaming in through the windows, and I wanted to be as far away from this place as I could. India might not be far enough. This is not geographical. (I have been a long-time subscriber to the belief that there is no such thing as a geographical cure.) Really, it's just that there is no longitude or latitude that will carry me far enough away from *me*.

It is not that I have lost myself. I have not. I discovered more facets of myself through my relationship with James (certainly, not all of them good) than I did with anyone else. Yet, I find that I do not know what I want, and my previous attempts to define it seemed to have resulted in miserable failures. I *thought* I knew. I really did. So I asked for it, quite blithely. And yet, here at the end, I realize that my wants became muddled, at best. They became a collection of mismatched items—gross contradictions. They devolved into bits and pieces of tattered things that do not fit together to form a coherent whole. This is what Ashrams are good for—battling the ego, fighting it with a gleaming sword until it is suitably chastened. Then, getting down to ground level and digging up the weeds so that you can actually see what you've got down there—whether you can plant anything in that soil or if it's pretty well drained of nutrients and you've got to burn everything and start again.

I had to pause in the middle of that thought to call a lawn service company. I maintained a very professional tone of voice while inquiring about their rates, which was amazing, considering that making the call made me want to weep. (Truthfully, *everything* makes me want to weep.) I am the mistress of this enormous house, whose total square footage I have no use for. I am the mistress of the lawn. I am the mistress of the bills. I am the mistress of three floors of emptiness.

Deal with it, I tell myself. *You will learn to love this house.*

Back to the rosebush. Josh reminds me that he has named his rosebush after me. I'm amazed that it's still alive, but that's the point. He says when he first bought his house (the Chickenshack, as he affectionately calls it), the rosebush was so overwrought with weeds that he would have missed it had it not been for the fattest most beautiful blooms sticking up through the tangle. It was being choked out by all the things around it that were trying to take more than their fair share of space; yet there it was, just the same. Brave little thing. He always says I wasn't dealt a fair hand. Life gave me shit, and I used it for fertilizer. "Look at you," he says. "You own a business, and you kept it going through 9/11 *and* a recession. You're smart. You're funny. You're beautiful. You're generous. Most people, coming from your background, would have turned out shit. But *you*, you turned out roses."

I nod my head. "That's nice of you to say," but what I really mean is, *I am that rare rose that is 100% thorn.*

Actually, I don't feel like vegetation at all. I feel like Frodo. I feel like I've carried a ring to Mount Doom, and I've thrown it in (but really, I didn't—because I was still kind of planning on keeping it all along), and now, I'm just standing there in a daze, expecting that those massive jets of lava or the collapsing rock will finish me off, and really, that feels A-Okay. "Here at the end of all things," right? (This is, I realize, an absurdly melodramatic thing to think. But a breakup is incredibly fertile soil for melodrama.)

So, the ring is destroyed. Now is the return to normal life. Only, that's impossible. I'm not Samwise. I will have to go off with the Elves. I have seen too much, and carrying that ring has changed my heart forever.

SONG OF THE LEAFBLOWER

I WOKE UP to the sound of a weed wacker, a lawn mower, and finally, a leaf blower. While normally I might find these to be terribly obnoxious sounds to wake up to, truly, in that moment I felt a bit giddy over them.

The day before, I'd been out on my incredibly tiny back porch, sitting in my chair watching the sun go down. The leaves are beginning to change color, and above the roof of my neighbor's garage, there is a giant tree that is slowly turning beautiful. I admit, for a second, I was actually able to breathe.

Feeling the last warm winds of summer, I am grateful that the weather has turned nice enough to allow for this quiet rumination. That's what I'm thinking when I finally get up, tea mug in hand, to head back inside.

Then I hear someone calling out, "Hey!"

It's my neighbor on the other side—the one who never talks to me. Suddenly, here he is, talking to me.

We commence to screaming at each other over the fence line. I always wondered why it seemed like he had only one volume of voice. I'm beginning to believe it's because he's not got the best hearing. Plus, attempts at conversation are being defeated by an airplane passing by overhead. Normally, I would use this as an excuse to smile politely, wave, and duck back inside. This time, I waited it out.

"Nice weather," I say. Because that's what you say to your neighbor.

He and his buddy agree. We also agree that it's going to stick around for at least a week, and that this is a good thing. We determine that we have in common the notion that winter sucks. We're not looking forward to winter. He throws up his hands and says, "Well, you know what I do for a living, right?"

I nod. Indeed I do. He owns a landscaping business. Not much winter work—and the light bulb goes off.

"Yeah," I say. "Actually, I've been trying to find someone to mow my lawn. We don't have a mower." (The "we" slips in unconsciously, although I'm conscious of it once it exits my mouth. It's true: "We" don't have a mower. We also no longer have a "we.")

"—we don't have a mower, and I can't seem to get any of these lawn service people to call me back with an estimate." This is true. Jerks!

He throws up his hands, as if he's offended by the very idea, the very *notion* that I have been calling lawn services. It's like I'm cheating on him.

"First thing in the morning," he says. "I'll do it first thing."

My gratitude is immediate and very, very real. "Really?" I say. "I can pay . . ."

He shakes his head. "You're my *neighbor*," he says. As if this should be enough. He tells me he mows the lawn across the street. (I'm aware. They don't deserve it. He has to mow around aluminum cans of Molson and a beer pong table.)

"First thing," he says again. "I'm Roy, by the way. And you're family."

And yes. By now I'm sure you know, in my fragile emotional state, these words made me a little watery-eyed. I went inside, closed the door, and felt a little less alone. I marveled at the idea that it took this event to open me to *everything* going on here. The little lady from down the street out walking in her orthopedic shoes and beige, knee-high stockings, so small and frail it breaks your heart. She has Alzheimer's, a recently deceased husband, and almost no family. There is only a church friend to watch over her—a woman whom, most times, she doesn't remember. "There's a lady who's always in my house," she complains, sometimes to strangers on the street. "I don't know who she is."

Seeing her, I am ashamed by the shallowness of my own suffering.

So, this morning, waking to the sound of the mower, I felt... something I could not describe. Perhaps gratitude mixed in with the grief. Unfortunately, there is something more lurking beneath that—I suspect it's something like…frustration. It doesn't feel quite peaceful. It feels wild…tumultuous, like a rumbling from some earthen pit. It feels like something that will erupt, punch through the earth in the form of a giant hand, grabbing hold of me and shaking me to bits. I call it *frustration* only because I don't want to call it anger. I want to dress up that rabid wolf in sheep's clothing so that I can seem more pious. I see the teeth anyway, poking out from beneath the cap of that snowy white wool. Teeth good for only one thing: gnawing at my insides—the kind of gnawing you get when you want so desperately for someone to SEE. "If only you'd SEEN," I want to shout. But it will do no good. Seen what? Me? Love? Hope? The capital "T" truth about his own wounded parts? It makes no difference. He saw what he saw, both of me and of himself. Who can say that these myopic eyes of mine were any better?

Still, *"No one will love you like I did,"* says the sad voice in my head, knowing he will not hear it; knowing that it's true. Knowing that, evidently, that wasn't what he needed anymore because here we are.

Without a we.

KRYPTONITE CIRCUS CAROUSEL TRAIN WRECK

REMEMBER THAT SCENE in *Superman Returns* (the yummiest Superman of all, in my opinion), where Superman confronts Lex Luthor on the continent he has sprouted using the crystals of Krypton? You see that first bead of sweat on Superman's brow, and you know he's in trouble. It turns out that Luthor, mastermind villain that he is, has embedded Kryptonite in the structure of the continent, and Superman is beginning to feel the effects.

That was how I spent my night—with Kryptonite. There was that first telltale bead of sweat, and then, all of a sudden, I could be knocked around again. (I mean this figuratively rather than literally, but it hurt just the same.)

It all began with a text message from James. In his text, I could detect a tone that was edging into desperation. After all, it was the second one he'd sent, and *why* wasn't I responding? He was finally serious about reaching me. He was finally *pleading.*

Only he was pleading to come by and get his upright bass, which he'd left behind.

"*Seriously,*" he writes. "I have a gig coming up."

Magically, the Mother Teresa slash Gandhi slash Buddha reserve I had been so carefully cultivating disappeared. Replacing it was that wolf with the nasty teeth. The thing I don't want to call anger but which is—let's face it, folks—*most definitely anger.*

I see, I think. *He doesn't come begging for the WOMAN he left behind; he comes begging for the BASS he left behind.* Bass isn't even his primary instrument. It's the thing that makes money on the side. It's *moonlighting.* And, I think, this pretty well sums up the relationship. I am second string to a Palatino four-string. Lovely as she is, I'd just as soon not compete with a piece of maple.

And yet—

that didn't matter once he was sitting in front of me. That's the way Kryptonite works. You are very strong until you get around it, and then you are very weak. Your very superhero-hotness drains out of you, and you're vulnerable to being pushed around. In this case, that meant that after we were done having the unpleasant but necessary discussion about the dispensation of possessions that might fall into the gray areas in terms of ownership (such as, what if I paid for the materials but he made the fill-in-the-blank object?), then we were on to a bunch of silence.

Silence.

S i l e n c e.

The kind of silence that always killed me before. The kind of silence that is a blade of Kryptonite, just like the one Lex Luthor jammed into Superman's side before shoving him off the edge of a cliff and into the ocean to drown.

This kind of silence always left me leaning *forward*, toward him, reaching out, saying, *Come on, please give me something to work with here.* As in,

feeling.

I suppose I was waiting for him to break down, look miserable, and tell me how much he missed me. That I'm all he can think about. That he's made a terrible mistake and suddenly realizes that he really *does* want to be with me.

That's what I was waiting for in that interminable silence.

There, in the heart-shriveling quiet, I realized that it was not I who ended things with him; it was the other way around. Yes, I said the words. They came from my mouth. But he'd always been the idea man to my implementer. Perhaps it allowed him an easier out. It afforded him the opportunity to say, "She asked me to leave." People will be sympathetic. "Oh, I'm so sorry to hear that!" they will say. But he will most likely fail to mention his innumerous behaviors that brought about our demise: "I told her I wasn't in love with her. She still stayed for another year after that, so I had to step it up a bit. I made sure to be there as little as possible. I stopped paying bills and buying food. Then I told her to 'shut the fuck up' and 'quit being a princess' when she expressed her displeasure over my increasingly unfriendly behavior."

In my defense, your honor, after he told me he wasn't in love with me, he explained that it was a matter of semantics. Please, all you young ladies out there: if a man ever tells you this, or that he would be in love with you except he has to "learn to be in love with life first," run away! Quickly! Don't look back. Run as if there were Giant Norwegian Trolls chasing you, or telemarketers, or whatever else scares the total shit out of you!

This is a glimpse into the ugly underbelly of Relationship. It's hard to bear witness to someone else's train wreck (regardless of all the rubbernecking we can't help but do)—especially when we accidentally catch a glimpse of a bone sticking out of an arm or a piece of glass jutting from someone's neck. A friend of mine once told me he saw someone decapitated in a roadside accident. "You don't ever get that picture out of your head," he said. Well, this isn't a decapitation, but it *is* the rather ugly business of making something dead. No matter how friendly it is, it's bound to get just a little *un*friendly. Even Nelson Mandela, who endured the persecution of apartheid and spent twenty-seven years in prison, suffered a very public divorce. His personal anguish was made a matter of record when he noted that his wife had been having an affair. He took the stand to say he had been "the loneliest man" upon his return from prison. This strikes me as especially heartbreaking. He wasn't the loneliest man *in* prison—he had to come home to his wife for that.

"Ladies and Gentlemen, step right up! Be Amazed. Not for the faint of heart. Welcome to the Death of Relationship!

As you might have guessed, this is definitely *not* the Greatest Show on Earth. The acrobats all miss the net.

DON'T YOU DARE QUOTE BOBBY MCFERRIN

I WOKE UP missing him. Terribly. I woke up staring at the corner garden in my living room, the sun struggling to stream in past the slats of the venation blinds, and as usual, I failed to experience even one sliver of a feeling of lightness or gratitude for being awake.

This is torture, I think. I know I will move past it (will I?). But in the beginning, it's torture. Plus, it's hard not to torture others with your torture. My best friend and I had been texting back and forth the night before, and there was no rosebush pep talk this time. "Relax," he wrote. "Jeesus...just be happy."

I wanted to write back, "Screw you, asshole!" But, I didn't. That's not a very nice thing to say to a friend, but come on. It's Day 5. That's what you say to someone who's on Day *365*. "Remind me," I texted back, "to be surly and pragmatic when you're upset about some girl who's not returning your phone calls." After all, this relationship had been serious, whereas he might be inclined to text me in crisis mode should the barmaid refuse to fall in love with him after one night of spooning.

"Just pull through," he wrote. "Don't wallow. Be happy."

"For the love you bear me," I typed back, "and all that is sacred in the heavens, Please. Stop. Saying. That."

I get it. No one wants to see me suffering this way. But there's a chemical component here. My body is actually going through a withdrawal of sorts. That soupy blend of dopamine, serotonin, norepinephrine, adrenaline, and phenylethylamine that is associated with falling in love is waning, then absent, and what does it all mean?

It means I might suddenly become a bit of a bummer. In his favor, he did at least respond with a joke:

What did the elephant say to the naked man?
How do you breathe out of something so small?

Later that day, I was reminded again of why social networking during this time is a bad idea. You get to experience the inevitable removal of yourself from your no-longer-significant-other's relationship status. This happened to be that day for me. *How did I know?* you ask, since it should be cardinal rule number one never to go to their Facebook page. Well, it turns out that Facebook was kind enough to inform me.

You have Notifications!
You know that guy with whom you were, like, "In a Relationship"?
Not anymore.
(Wanna play a little Candy Crush?)

Don't wallow, right? Just be happy.

Only, it felt like someone had sort of mucked about in my body so that all of my organs were now on the *outside*—right before shoving me into a cactus.

Now what?

Now it's time to put myself in Relationship Revisionist Recovery. (I can't take credit for this term. You can thank authors Greg Behrendt and Amiira Ruotola; it was noted in their book, *It's Called A Breakup Because It's Broken*.) Relationship Revisionism is where you look back over your relationship wearing six pairs of rose-colored glasses. All of a sudden, you've forgotten all of the bad parts. You're thinking about how it was in the beginning, and not how it was near the end—for instance, all those things that totally and completely sucked or that made you want to scoop out portions of your brain (or his) with a melon baller.

What does this recovery involve, you ask? (Aside from every single one of your friends and family members telling you that it sucked and "You're better off and remember that time he fill-in-the-blank or that other time when you complained about fill-in-the-blank, and all that other fill-in-the-blank stuff you hated and that made you cry and feel incredibly sad and lonely and that tortured us because we were the ones who had to listen to you complain and/or cry?") Yeah, well, aside from *that*, I made a list. I made *two* lists. What I disliked about James, and what I loved. I'd made lists before, mind you, while *in* the actual relationship. But I'd always managed to skew them in favor of sticking it out. Because. Duh. That's what you do when you're in love.

This time, I urged myself to be nitpicky. I listed every little thing I didn't like. Some were small—things that you can (and probably should) absolutely get over. They are not deal breakers. But others were HUGE, monumental, absolute, and all-kinds-of-ridiculous deal breakers, and…ahem…that list was rather long.

The list that detailed the things I loved? Surprisingly short this time; however, no less potent for its brevity. To quote Greg Behrendt again, *"It doesn't matter how much mayonnaise you add—you can't make chicken salad out of chicken shit."* But dammit, I was still going to try.

It's amazing how Relationship Revisionism works that way. You can have three pages full of the bad, but those three paragraphs of good? Well, I mean, they were *really, really good, right!? You'll never find anyone who can do those three things as well as He could.*

You know what should go at the top of every list with the heading, "What is wrong with this picture?" There should be something like, "He broke up with me," or, "I broke up with him" (however it happened). There was a reason. No fair calling it a case of temporary insanity if you've been considering this notion for any length of time. Say…six months. I think that pretty well counts as premeditated.

It still sucks. Making lists sucks.

I bet he's not making any lists.

LAST NIGHT, I reached critical mass. I stumbled across a beautiful cover of the Don Henley song "Heart of the Matter," triggering an unexpected deluge. The tears receded quickly, but the damage had been done. The immediate and startling side effect: clogged ears. As in, my body had finally finished filling up my sinuses from a week's worth of tears and decided to move on to my ears as a secondary repository for fluid. Ouch!

This was torment. Advil did not help. Neither did saline nasal spray (in my nose, not my ears). I tried sitting in the bathroom with the shower running on full hot again. Ditto. No help there. Finally, I just gave up and did my best to deal with it. Still, I tossed and turned all night. There was no way to get comfortable. I would drift off for a moment and then snap back awake from dreams filled with vague indications of pain. The sky was lighter each time I opened my eyes.

The waking moments left plenty of time to think.

In one of these moments, it occurred to me that I didn't fall into the Naïve Girl trap—you know, the one where you try to *change* a man. I fell into the *other* Naïve Girl trap: the one where you think your love will magically transform all of his wounded bits into bacon bits. I mean, his weathered parts into *feathered parts*, which will allow him to sweep you off your feet and carry you to the heavens.

Because, quite naturally, my love is so amazingly stupendous and powerful and full of light that I could just shine it down a dark well and illuminate everything! "I see you down there in that well," beautiful princess girl says, "and now that I'm shining my light down there, you can see a way out, right?"

Let me tell you this: It doesn't work that way.

Naïve Girl wanted so desperately for him to break free from all of the things I felt were tying him down so he could accomplish what I knew he was capable of accomplishing—if only he would believe it as much as I did! If only he would open himself to the risk of being hurt, it would also mean opening himself up to the possibility of joy.

Oh, my dear girl, I think to myself. *You are sweet, but dumb.*

Over the years, he had perfected his various coping mechanisms for the *sameness* that permeated his life, the system of defenses and tactics; sentries, guards and walls; potions and pills for numbing, methods of distraction, modes of focus that would take him away from the things that had been unfair to him in life and bring him… respect, love, attention. He had figured out what worked for him. For me to suggest that this lifelong manner of handling his business was somehow inept or inefficient was…well, presumptuous. It was arrogant and absolutely irrelevant.

It must have been about me.

I wanted him to reach the potential that I saw in him because I thought it would make him happy. I thought he deserved good things after all the sad things that life had handed him. And I thought that if *he* were happy, he would then be able to turn his attention to *me*. If I could give him enough, if I could just contort myself enough so that he could use me as a springboard, then his success would bring me… not money, fortune, or shared glory, but *love*. And then we would finally be on the same page.

Such notions, often discussed during late-night inspirational pep talks (normally shared while I was sitting at the kitchen table drawing aimless swirls on our bamboo placemat with a ballpoint pen while he ate tortillas and peanut butter), fell on deaf ears. No matter how much we may love, no matter how healing and redeeming such love *can* be—we have to be open first. We have to love ourselves first. We have to be willing to be cracked open, broken down, rearranged, and totally *dissolved*. We have to know what we want and then be fearless enough to pursue it, and in the end, I was not. My love, once fearlessly given, turned frantic. Every step back he took led me to take two steps forward to fill the gap. *Where are you?* I wanted to say. *Where are you going?*

I was out of balance—climbing into my car in the middle of the night, shivering in the dark, pulling out of the driveway, wondering which direction to go. I was running the circuit of bars at 3 a.m., worried, feeling like a crazy woman. *I am **not** the kind of woman who gets in a car and drives around looking for her man,* I thought, driving around looking for my man.

No matter what, he *liked* how things were. He *liked* the wild unpredictability of his life. He liked such freedom—the freedom to be exactly as he was. Not trying to change him and thinking I could transform his pain were simply two sides of the same coin—albeit, one side gave the bullshit a bit of a fancier finish.

He was never the one with the problem.

I was.

Which means this: If I'm going to be the little lantern girl, I'd better shine that light into my *own* dark well and say,

"You can see a way out, right?"

PULL FORWARD, PLEASE

DOES THE UNIVERSE have some sort of grand design, or is this all just terribly random chaos? I'm a part of this universe, right? My molecules are spinning around same as yours, interacting, intersecting with everything, so I should get some say. I should have some word in how things turn out.

That's what I woke up thinking on Day Seven, suddenly desperate to fathom the nature of the universe. At one point in time, I thought I knew. (Yep. I was pretty sure I had this whole "understanding the universe" thing on lockdown.) I was happy, and healthier, and on a creative high. I felt good about the life I was building. I was alone, yes, but I was sending out all that "positive energy," saying things like, "Universe, I am picturing this *Insert Description Here* thing in my life." And of course, according to all those "The Secret" folks out there, the universe had received my order, wearing its World's Best Chef apron and telling me to pull around to the next window. If I just drove forward a bit, I would be able to reach out and pick up my fill-in-the-blank. In this case, I'd special-ordered a husband, with whom I would be deeply and passionately in love and who would also, of course, be deeply and passionately in love with me. *Wait! With a side order of We INSPIRE Each Other,* added for good measure. I wanted to *grow* together! None of this stagnant, "let's just agree to be screwed up and never do anything about it" crap.

Not long after I began saying this prayer, ta-da! In walked a man with whom I fell most *definitely* deeply, passionately in love. I was in the deep end of the pool. I couldn't touch bottom, and I was perfectly fine with that, even without water wings. No flotation devices. So what if I couldn't swim? For this guy, I'd doggie-paddle to Pluto.

It didn't matter that I was there in the deep end first.

I had FAITH.

I had HOPE.

I had BELIEF.

And eventually, he fell in…

well, I mean, I *thought* he fell in…

but really, he just kind of dipped his toes in, and then walked down the stairs into the shallows, and then…

he kind of swam around near to where I was, and then away again, and then near, and then away . . .

and then…

let's face it.

The universe got my order wrong.

There aren't any refunds. I can't take it back and complain about how I'll never patronize this establishment again because it's the ONLY ESTABLISHMENT. There's no escaping the universe, and there's no escaping my desire to give and receive love—which means I'll be back. I'll be back to pick up that hand-wrapped heart attack. *But*, I'll be back already assuming I'm going to get swindled. Why? Because what more could I have said? What part of "Hold the mayonnaise, pickle, and bullshit" didn't it get? Why did it mess things up so royally when I tried so hard to be specific?

Turns out, it was probably my fault after all. I didn't go into this "asking the universe" business thinking it should give me whatever it thought would best fit the bill. This divinely inspiring and passionately loving husband I'd requested, well…I didn't just put it out there that the universe should find one and bring him to me. I sort of…well, I sort of already had someone in mind. I just assumed, I suppose, that the universe would *know* I had someone in mind, and would steer me clear if he didn't match up with what I'd been asking for.

But the universe did not.

So, I proceeded to get what I asked for *in action*. Yes, if you want to know the truth of it, I had one of those Oprah and The Secret People wish boards in my living room. It was small, a lowly little corkboard really, but I'd put a bunch of stuff on it. A check for a lot of money, and some other things I can barely remember (which means they weren't really all that important) and then, dead center, a picture that had been taken of James and me together outside of the Blues benefit concert I mentioned before—our first time seeing each other since right after high school. In that moment when the picture was taken, it was as if no time had passed. I knew him; I knew that he was the one for me and that I was the one for him. I knew it right then, posing for that picture—knew it bone deep. He was it. I adored him already.

But, I let it go. (Not really.) I thought I was putting it into the hands of the universe. (Nope.) If it was to be, then so be it. But there I was with a picture of us on my corkboard and a picture of him in my head when I started saying my prayers for this divine husband of mine.

Him, him, let it be him, I was practically chanting. *But, I mean, whoever you think* (but it's HIM), *I mean, whatever you think is best* (as long as it's HIM).

I mean, how was I supposed to know that the universe would let it happen if it wasn't supposed to be *him*?

This is tricky. It happened, which meant it *was* supposed to happen. It *was* what I wanted, because I'd wished for it awfully hard, hadn't I? I had asked for it, and like the old adage says, "Be careful what you wish for. You might just get it."

And it wasn't right. Half of it was right—the part where I loved. The other part, where it was returned? Not so much. Really, it's embarrassing. I mean, finding out that you're no big deal to the person you thought invented sunshine and streusel coffeecake is sort of... appalling, really. It's a very large blow to one's sense of rightness with the world.

What it leaves is this:

How do you get out of the way? How do you *not* have something in mind when you're asking for something? Isn't it fair to have a picture in your head?

I used to pray things like, "Please help me to reach a state of peace and calm with whatever happens." That prayer pretty well covers everything. That's a very reasonable prayer. That means if someone is handing me flowers or stabbing me in the arm repeatedly with a fork, I'm maintaining a sense of calm—equilibrium. It's all good, baby.

This is also how I managed to stay in my relationship—because it doesn't *have* to be good all the time. Nothing is good *all* the time. Perhaps my job was to find out what it was like to love so much in a very one-sided way. And yes, that is exactly right, because that's what happened. I found out what it was like. Did I reach a state of peace and calm with it? No, and I can't say I don't feel like a failure over it. It was an unanswered prayer, to be calm about all that unhappiness.

Is it okay to want to be happy? Not just calm, but happy? Is it possible?

James used to answer "no" to that question. We can't be happy as people. It's all about suffering. At the time, I agreed with him. I thought, it *is* all about suffering. But I also thought that it was about making peace with that fact—making peace with each other regardless of the suffering, maybe even wrapping ourselves and each other and *everyone* in the arms of compassion *because* of it.

We never did that. We never could.

But the suffering I am experiencing now is all on me. The arms that are left, the arms that have the job of wrapping me up in compassion…are my own.

FIRST QUARTER
(MONTHS 1 – 3)

CHAPTER 1

Upon Returning to an Empty House

I'd left town. That seemed the sensible thing to do given the Kryptonite experience I'd had before. The deal was that I would leave and this would give James time to move out his belongings. All of them. There would be none of that "you can store your stuff here until you find a place to put it" arrangement he'd had with a previous girlfriend. I didn't want him stopping by for some random item from some random box at some random time. It might be too tempting for me to throw myself at his feet and beg him to come back.

When the week was up, I entered the house, heart pounding, steeling myself against all the evidence of his absence. In the dining room, for instance, the bar stools were gone. Also, the kitchen floor was *filthy*. The cracking grout lines were stained dark brown and the back door mat was crusted over with dried mud—two things that were very evident with all the light spilling into the kitchen from the open back door.

Ugh, wait. The open back door?

Yes, *wide open*, like a gaping mouth, like an accusation, like a punch in the gut. Not a little bit open. A lot open. All the way open. As in, "Don't bother with your lock pick tools, Mr. Burglar, I've conveniently *Left The Door Open*."

My mother, who'd come in with me for moral support, was practically frothing at the mouth—not about the mud but about the back door. Anyone could have come in. They could have cleaned me out. "He did it on purpose," she said.

"No, I doubt that," I replied. That is, when I could draw breath enough to speak.

"He did it on purpose by virtue of being a thoughtless asshole," she added.

Well…she's got me there, I thought.

She was already calling for her husband—presumably so that he could check the house and deal with whatever crazed madman might, even now, be building a nest in the basement out of cardboard boxes and dryer lint. Her voice held the heightened tension of barely-contained anger. If James had been standing there, she would have taken the toaster oven she was holding and landed it squarely on top of his head.

But I wasn't waiting. This was my opportunity. It's easy to be brave in grief, because the only real consolation is the thought of…well, death.

I strode purposely into the basement, *hoping* some madman was down there with a chainsaw waiting to hack away at my limbs.

No such luck. Instead—

The basement was empty of his belongings. Gone were his work tools and bench and the empty beer bottles from his home brewing kit. The seats from his van were conspicuously absent, as was the gear he used to tote to gigs.

In fact, the only thing left was a lone box of plates, a simple blue pattern on porcelain. The box was easy enough to carry up to the porch and dump over the edge of the railing into the open mouth of the dumpster. Ah! The satisfying sound of dishware shattering!

But there was no would-be ax-murderer.

Just mud.

Then, upstairs, all that reversal of overcrowded confusion that had been his practice room was reduced to a lone carpet and—because it was mine to begin with—a faux suede stool with a broken leg. In the corner, propped up, was the Pièce *de* résistance: the acoustic guitar I had given him years ago when I first found out he didn't have one. That was back when love was new, and it was sacrilegious that I should have this instrument that could be better brought to life in his capable hands. After all, he had been first chair at his music school. He was a professional! He just didn't have one because he was broke. Broke and living with his mother.

There it was now, in the corner, left behind with the dog bed and little green squeaky frog I'd bought his dog, and what the hell was I going to do with either one?

It was all bad, but truly my mind kept going back and forth between the guitar, propped up in the corner, and the mud on the kitchen floor—the way the grime had been ground into the mat by the door. I would never get that out of the fibers. I broke down right there, sliding down to the tile and sobbing out the injustice of having had my heart so completely broken.

Reality. He was gone…except for his prized Joshua Tree mug, which he'd left on the second shelf in the cabinet. It was a souvenir from his time spent hiking in the desert as a high school senior, and getting lost, and maybe almost dying…and if he *had* died, well…I would have been spared this moment. Right? Only that's a terrible thought to be having. Absolutely un-Zen.

No, that mug was a precious artifact. I knew how much it had meant to him. I vowed right then and there to leave it where it was. Maybe someday I would return it. Until then, I would simply never look on the second shelf again for any reason.

But why would he leave the aftershave in the bathroom? Oh, right. Because I'd bought it for him. Otherwise, there was no trace of him remaining. Had he been there at all? I wished there was some doubt, but there were those muddy prints to contend with on that kitchen floor mat, and there were those tire tracks in the back yard, another metaphor for what I thought he had done to my heart (namely, driven across it a few hundred times in his minivan).

Thinking about that back door, I wanted to call him. I wanted to blame him. "You left the door open!" I would pretend that his lackluster apology could apply to the way he had left me feeling about *everything*, but what I really wanted to do was beg him to bring it all back. I only meant for us to take a break, not break up, or out, or over, or through, and certainly not to end like this: without a word, except that guitar propped against the wall.

I shut the door to that room like someone had died. Well, someone *had* died. It was just that I was still walking around.

It gets much worse.

CHAPTER 2
A PICTURE'S WORTH A THOUSAND WORDS (AND FACEBOOK WILL LIKELY MAKE YOU WANT TO PLUCK OUT YOUR EYEBALLS)

REMEMBER THAT MUG? The one I said I would leave where it was? Well, that was until THIS happened. When THIS happened, I decided that I would most certainly *not* leave that mug where it was. I would relocate it—to a Glad ForceFlex garbage bag, and then bang that bag rather furiously against the previously mud-laced tile until I was satisfied that what was left was something the consistency of desert sand. Sayonara, precious artifact!

Why did I do this?

Facebook.

It is easiest to blame it on Mark Zuckerberg and his evil brainchild, perfect for stalkers who don't want to bother with leaving the house. No binoculars required. No crazy drive-bys in the middle of the night. The scope of spying is far and wide. You can see his page, his family, his friends, any hour of the day or night…just as long as you don't mind a little self-torture. Masochism at its finest. I mean, we'd already done the ritual of removing each other from our Facebook relationship status. But that didn't mean I didn't still go to his page.

It went something like this:

Visit 1

In place of my name in the "In a Relationship" spot, he'd placed a woman named Lisa in the category of "cousin." Lisa was a married woman who had a crush on him. I'd always teased him about it, and he always knew that this teasing was edging right up to the border of me being jealous. So, what kind of ridiculous shenanigan was this? He could care less about her! She was married! Why would she have consented to be listed as his cousin in the first place? We were all devolving into teenagers, it seemed. This was a jab at my ribcage with a sharp stick.

Visit 2

I found myself offended by his profile picture. It was a picture of him with his recently shaved head. I'd been the one to shave it. I'd also been the one to take the picture. Irrationally, I was irritated that he should still be using a picture I'd taken. I mean, didn't he have the decency to attach all sorts of associations to such things? That picture should make him think of me... and then miss me, and...and... Worse than ignoring the proper protocol for feeling miserable, there he was exhibiting Chatty Kathy characteristics online, even though he could have cared less about Facebook in the past. Clearly, he was desperately filling holes. (See how superior that sounded? I reiterate, devolving...)

Visit 3

Disaster. Mountains are crumbling. Skies are falling. My heart seems to have crept up somewhere in the vicinity of my throat. This is not an ideal location for it to be. He has been sharing political posts from someone named Sara. I wish this were a foreign name. I wish I had no idea whatsoever who this person is. Unfortunately, I know EXACTLY who it is.

It is his ex-girlfriend.

The one who cheated on him.

Worse.

The one he had once been in love with—the crazy sort of love where you feel half-sick whenever you're around that person. (You know, the kind I'd had for him.)

Even worse.

Sara was the one he thought maybe he could have married. She was the one who got away. (You know...uh...like how I felt about him.)

She had been the topic of conversation on certain nights. I would sit at the kitchen table, watching him eat peanut butter and tortillas or roast beef and tortillas or just about anything and tortillas. "You're sure you wouldn't rather have *that?*" I would ask. "That crazy kind of love?"

"Of course not," he assured me. (*I'd much rather keep on feeling tepid about you*, was what I couldn't help hearing.)

And yet.

Here she was.

Here.

Only.

Two weeks.

Later.

Which, of course, begs the question of how long she'd been in the picture *before* that, which sets the horror level on something like TEN MILLION.

To say I went ballistic over this would not have been accurate. (See below for ballistic.)

Visit 4

(Hint. Stop while you're ahead. Really. Don't keep going to his page. But since you probably will anyway, until something horrible kills you, picture me holding your hand right now.)

Since there was…uh…yeah…I mean *she* was on his page, and there, where her name was, was a link to *her* page . . .

(Don't do it!)

Click!

Shit. Shit. Shit. Shit. Shit.

If all that had come before seemed somewhat torturous, then I was grossly mistaken. That had been nothing compared to this.

Her profile picture was the two of them together, snuggled up, very cozy—and on her own page, she'd written that she was blissfully happy, with little heart symbols trailing after. (Little heart symbols? Really?) He was wearing a sweater I'd bought him, his head pressed tightly against her head, his arm around her.

This is what it feels like to have a bomb enter your eyeballs and explode in your chest. This is the sort of image that burns itself into your brain forever and ever and ever. For the next month (no exaggeration), I fell asleep with this image in my head, I woke up with this image in my head…it would pop into my consciousness at random points throughout the day. Suddenly, I was thinking of the movie *Eternal Sunshine of the Spotless Mind*. I wanted to erase that picture from my memory. I wanted to erase *him* from my memory. Us. Everything. A frontal lobotomy would have been perfectly acceptable. I didn't want this in my head. I would have given anything to un-see it. Anything. I would *still* give anything to un-see it. Even my friends (to whom I so graciously forwarded this little nugget) would like to un-see it.

Moral:

After the breakup, immediately block him. Immediately. Unless you are having a very amiable and friendly breakup, don't wait. Block family. Block friends. Block the page he made for his dog (seriously, he made a page for his dog, and I had to block it). Block every possible portal because if you don't, you will stumble across something that will saw you in two. You will wish you could pluck out everything inside of you and replace it with straw, and then douse that in gasoline, and then light a match. Any equilibrium you might have been gaining can be shattered in an instant when something like this occurs. I don't care how Zen you feel. Seeing that will remind you of how very, very far you are from Buddhahood. It's excellent fodder for practice, I'll give you that. But really, there isn't any need to add this much insult to injury.

After that incident, I found myself spending an inordinate amount of time crouched on the floor, sobbing. There was nothing more that could be done. I had a complete and total breakdown.

There's a pureness there, but it takes a special kind of bravery to abandon yourself to that pain. It's scary; that much pain feels like it will kill you. Very seriously, there are certain depths of hurt that make you feel as if you can't continue on with life. You are well aware of the saying that death, in this case, would be a permanent solution to a temporary problem. The trouble with this is that *it doesn't feel like a temporary problem*—at least not while you're right in the moment. It can be hard to get through that, and if you're feeling that way, there is no shame in seeking help. This could be church, a counselor, therapist, or suicide counselor. (I chose to see a spiritual counselor. My grief was extensive enough that I required an impartial third party to talk to.) But the other important thing is to surrender to the grief when it comes. It will come, and then it will pass for a bit. Consider it a griefquake, or like the tide coming in (and drowning you) before going back out. (No, really…it's like being waterboarded.) But each time, you will be a little bit more broken down. Your structures will be less defined. Your walls will begin to break apart. I know. These things all sound bad, at first, but remember that bit about dissolution and growth? In the end, the grief will wash you clean, if you are strong enough to let it.

(Told you not to click that.)

Equation to Calculate the Degree to Which an Event is Torture

$$a \div b \times 100 = \textit{Degrees of Torture}$$

In other words:

The (a) action in which the party is engaged ÷ (b) the length of time since the breakup (in weeks) × perceived happiness quotient of the offending party (this is a set value of 100. I mean, they never seem less than 100% happy, right?) = degrees of torture.

Sample Actions in Which the Party May be Engaged:

a. Not contacting you, even though he should be. I mean, not even so much as a drunk dial? Not even a late-night text where he's raging against the injustice of your very ability to breathe or begging you to take him back because he was a fool to have let you go? **Score 25**

b. Removing you from his Facebook status. This is inevitable, best done quickly, like ripping off a Band-Aid. All right. I fully admit, it feels more like digging a bullet out of your rib cage with a hot fork using sulfuric acid as antiseptic. **Score 50**

c. Random flirtatious and/or vague and obnoxious cryptic Twitter postings. Is he posting random comments like, "Thought you could win my heart in your crackerjack box, but I got the decoder ring"? **Score 75**

d. Hooking up with some random new chick. I'm not sure how you would know this, but let's assume you do, since turning into a stalker is pretty much part of the breakup process. Said chick is some drunk girl he met in a bar. Most likely, it's about purging you from his system. It's meaningless to him. It's torturous to you. **Score 150**

e. Hooking up with an ex. The familiar is the easiest thing in the world to go back to. It's safe. It's known. It's comfortable. It also makes you want to remove your heart from your chest—or his—with plastique explosives. **Score 500**

f. Hooking up with an ex he was in love with before you (who also cheated on him and then dumped him and then wanted him back but he was already with you when she figured this out—*this is totally hypothetical, of course*). This is tantamount to someone setting off an atom bomb in the base of your spine. There is no number that can describe this, but this is fake math, so we'll say **Score 1,000**

That would make my personal equation look something like this:

$$1{,}000 \div 2 \text{ (weeks)} \times 100 = 50{,}000 \text{ Degrees of Torture}$$

For perspective, the Earth's mantle, at its deepest point, is only about 7,230 °F.

Clearly, this is some awful business, but this awful business also has real *science* behind it—and that's what we're going to look at next.

LET'S LANCE THIS boil and drain out some of the romance, shall we?

There are lots of chemicals interacting with each other when we fall in love. It is Nature's Own Cocktail for keeping us alive and reproducing.

Initially, we're driven by sex hormones—testosterone and estrogen. Once we are love-struck, we are driven by neurotransmitters. Neurotransmitters are "brain chemicals that communicate information throughout our brain and body."[3] They serve an important purpose: telling our various body systems what to do. Lungs, breathe! Stomach, digest! Heart, beat! But they also impact our moods in significant ways. In both falling in love and breaking up, specific neurotransmitters are mixing up a potent chemical concoction comprised primarily of norepinephrine or adrenaline, dopamine, and serotonin. It always feels a little stressful falling in love, doesn't it? Compulsive. We can't help ourselves. Our heart races, our mouths go dry—and this is the reason.

Dopamine triggers a rush of pleasure. Neurochemically, it is connected to our "reward" centers. Thus, the more dopamine we release, which gives us that rush of pleasure, the more we feel we "have to have" whatever it is that is causing us to release that chemical in the first place. It's like taking cocaine (literally, *it has the same effect on the brain!*). There's a rush when we see or think about our beloved. Like speed, it increases our energy level and decreases our need for sleep (fueling all those late-night gab sessions where we feel like we may never need to sleep again). Everything is golden, brilliant, outlined in rose petals and fairy dust.

Enter serotonin. This neurotransmitter impacts our moods and our ability to be flexible. Lower levels cause us to fixate. We suddenly find that we can't get this particular person out of our heads. We may suffer from extremes of emotion. In a study of the brain chemistry of couples who considered themselves to be madly in love with each other, blood samples showed that their serotonin levels were equivalent to the low serotonin levels of those with obsessive-compulsive disorder. So when we say love is compulsive, well, that's because *it is*.

Epinephrine and norepinephrine are two chemicals produced in the adrenal glands, spinal cord, and the brain and are responsible for the adrenaline rush we seem to feel when we first fall in love. We are meant to focus in on the attraction and love feelings we are experiencing.

This potent combination of chemicals also takes other systems offline—for instance, the prefrontal cortex, which helps us in matters of judgment and impulse control. The neural circuits that deal with the way we assess others are also suppressed. In effect, we are love-blind. We are trip-trapping our way along, blind to all of the negative traits of our beloved so that we can move further along in relationship-building to an attachment stage—something that will outlast this chemical cocktail that's churning away inside of us, destined to fade. After all, there might be children who need raising.

Basically, the process of falling in love is a little (or a lot) like going crazy. Thankfully, this feeling doesn't last. This initial potent brew is meant to make way for other chemical concoctions, which enable us to settle in for the long haul.

Seratonin plays another role. As time passes, more balanced levels are reached. When this level is neither increased nor decreased, the result is lessened anxiety and aggression. We should no longer be fixated on a particular person or thing and should be able to entertain a wider focus.

Vasopressin is a chemical that is made in the brain. Although it is produced by both men and women, its effects are enhanced in men because it synergizes with testosterone. Vasopressin appears to impact male sexual behavior. In mammals, it promotes aggression and territorial competition. More importantly, perhaps, it is one component that seems to encourage male bonding with both their children and their mates—including monogamous behavior and feelings of protectiveness.

Oxytocin serves a function in women that is similar to vasopressin in men, synergizing with estrogen. This neuropeptide hormone helps to facilitate childbirth and nursing, but it also increases by large degrees during sex. For men, the levels increase dramatically during orgasm, which may be why they experience a feeling of closeness and bonding during sex; however, this effect does not last. Instead, after sex, vasopressin again increases in men. For women, the levels take longer to return to normal, which may explain a woman's desire for continued touch and closeness even after the act. Oxytocin increases our desire for bonding, nurturing, monogamy, and the protection of our children. Levels of oxytocin increase when we touch, and if this pattern of touch becomes consistent, levels will actually increase simply in *anticipation* of touch.

Armed with this information, we begin to see the role that brain chemistry plays both in the process of falling in love and in staying together after the initial chemical rush wears off, which may take up to 1 – 2 years. By understanding this process, we know that it is possible for the richness of love to be maintained over a longer course of time. A study examining the neural correlates of long-term romantic love showed that couples married an average of twenty-one years who still reported being deeply in love with each other showed activity in the regions of the brain associated with falling in love, including the dopamine reward system; but an important difference was that these couples did not exhibit activity in the regions of the brain associated with anxiety, which was the case for couples who were still in the early stages of falling in love. Instead, the brain activity of those in long-term, loving relationships was associated with regions of calm. Perhaps this was due to normal levels of serotonin. In addition, they may have been able to create intimacy through activities that increased the levels of vasopressin and oxytocin released (such as regular patterns of touching).

Now, what does all this mean for a broken heart?

A study published in the July 2010 edition of the *Journal of Neuro-physiology*[4] examined the emotional regulation systems associated with the ending of relationships where one partner professed to still be very in love with his or her ex. They examined the brains of 10 women and 5 men who had recently suffered the rejection of their partners. The areas impacted were similar to the areas impacted when one is falling in love—essentially the reward centers, craving, addiction, and emotional regulation.

The participants in the study all acknowledged the typical intense emotional anxieties that accompany a painful breakup—obsessive thinking about their ex-partner; feelings of intense despair; the longing to reconcile; frequent contact with their ex in an attempt to reconcile; self-destructive behaviors, such as drinking too much; and a general lack of emotional control, including difficulty functioning in their daily lives. Sound familiar?

Those who were shown pictures of ex-partners with whom they were still in love showed activity in the regions of the brain associated with the same motivation/reward system as those in love, but also those associated with cravings and addiction, along with physical pain. In addition, there were increases in regions involved with assessing behavior and controlling emotions. (Let's add that up: withdrawal, motivation to win back our love, assessing past behavior in a near-obsessive manner, and physical pain. Yes, this sounds like a breakup!)

In addition, they found that the length of the relationship did not necessarily impact the degree of brain activity in the regions mea-sured—which is different from those who are in happy, long-term relationships, where the length of the relationship helps to calm some of the more "intense" effects of the love experience.

So, essentially, when we profess to still be "in love" with partners who no longer want us, we are left with the regions of the brain that led us to love in the first place, still firing off that potent brew of chemicals—however, rather than receiving the "reward" of that person's presence and returned affection (firing off dopamine to make us feel all warm and fuzzy), there is simply a void. This leads us to the intense craving sensation, with all of the attendant obsessive-compulsive impulses and goal-oriented behaviors that demand we win back our lost love. The regions of the brain impacted are the same regions impacted by drug addictions.

The good news is that regions of the brain that seek to regulate emotions and learn from them in order to control behavior are also activated. This may indicate that in our pain, we are still seeking a form of resolution, a way to LEARN from this experience in order to manage our despair—essentially evaluating gains and losses, involving ourselves in positive reassessment of negative emotional stimuli, and using that goal-oriented drive to accomplish *new* goals.

The study concluded that it may be possible to reduce some of these intense feelings via cognitive therapy approaches—in addition to encouraging "recently rejected individuals to actively recall the events that led to the dissolution of the relationship, rather than 'ruminating' on their pain…"[5]

It may also be helpful to recall that the chemicals vasopressin and oxytocin, which play a role in the strength of our attachments, will lessen as time passes and we have less contact with our ex-partner. This will decrease the feelings that led us to experience pair-bonding with this individual.

Science has also shown that the pain of a broken heart, or emotional pain, is processed in the same area of the brain as *physical* pain. In a three-week trial at the University of California,[6] 62 people were told to take Tylenol or a placebo and then record their feelings each night. The results? The study showed that those who took 1,000mg of the OTC painkiller showed a reduction in their hurt feelings over those who took the placebo.

So, we can see that there are excellent, scientific reasons for why we feel so miserable! To some degree, we must wait out this chemical explosion—just as if we were overcoming an addiction to narcotics. Certainly this is also a good argument for ceasing all contact with your ex, at least in the initial stages, if this is possible and no children are involved. Imagine if you were suffering from a cocaine addiction, yet in your attempts to quit, you continued to take the drug *every once in a while*. Would this prolong your period of recovery? Absolutely!

It also means that in those moments when you absolutely *swear* you would do anything to be back with your ex-partner, even though deep down you know he or she is not right for you, it is because you are experiencing a range of wildly chaotic symptoms that are causing a momentary lapse in reason. Just as it was compulsive that you had to be with this person in the beginning, so it is again in the end. This may be why so many couples get back together after a breakup (which rarely works, by the way). It's hard to go cold turkey. This is also why so many people can only overcome one relationship by quickly getting into another. This serves to lessen or alleviate entirely the feelings of withdrawal, since the dopamine reward system is back online—simply with a different person providing the chemical feedback needed. While these things might help you with the *physical* symptoms, I would have to say that they do not do as much for your *spiritual and emotional growth*.

Eventually, time will lessen the strength of the brain activity that is heightening the misery of the situation. The feelings of attachment will recede. The craving and withdrawal will fade. In the meantime, it can be important for us to allow ourselves to experience this emotional pain as an important part of our development. The brain is capable of learning from this experience. Learning is a good thing, because while you might be inclined to swear off love for the time being, the chances are excellent that you will fall in love again someday.

Let's face it. We're hard-wired for this. We are built for joining, mating, reproducing...and nature's little trick for this appears to be encouraging insanity...*uhm*...I mean, *bonding*. Forming communities and partnerships are also part of what allows us to survive as a species, so as much as we might like to think we can turn into nuns and hermits, chances are, we're still longing for connection.

But in order to build and maintain strong partnerships, we must have something within us that helps us move past the initial thrill of falling in love. Once the chemicals wear off, and we're able to think clearly again, we have an excellent chance to see into ourselves and others.

The initial phases of love have a way of blinding us to the true wholeness of others. Of course, we understand this biological necessity, but there will come a day when the blinders come off. At that point, it is very helpful if we know ourselves and have reached a point in our lives where a love of reality can trump a love of fantasy.

> "To love another in spite of his weaknesses and errors
> and imperfections is not perfect love. No, to love is

to find him lovable in spite of and together with his weaknesses and errors and imperfections....It is a sad upside-downness, altogether too common, to talk on and on about how the object of love should be before it can be loved. The task is not to find the lovable object, but to find the object before you lovable."
- Søren Aabye Kierkegaard

But there is a caveat: I spent a good portion of my relationship working to change *myself* so that I might better fit to the "reality" of my situation. This means I re-evaluated my needs on a regular basis and then began to *reduce* and *devalue* them so that I could continue to tolerate that reality. Certainly I thought that this was part of finding the object before me lovable, but I was doing so by disengaging from the true needs of my own heart. This only works for so long. The reason is because when we continue to devalue our inherent needs, *when we begin to reduce ourselves as a person* in order to stay in a relationship, we are essentially agreeing to limit our potential and anesthetize our authentic self in the name of love or a sense of duty born of our investment in the connections we have formed.

In mature love, in order to reach a point where we can find the objects before us lovable, I feel that we must first focus on finding *ourselves* lovable. This means discovering the truth about our selves and our desires and then honoring this truth to the best of our ability. This is not so much a matter of choosing to leave a relationship because "you deserve to be loved the way you want to be loved" but because **you deserve to know and be who you truly are without self-reduction.** Kierkegaard also said, *"...in the world of spirit, busyness, keeping up with others, hustling hither and yon, makes it almost impossible for an individual to form a heart, to become a responsible, alive self.... True individuality is measured by this: how long or how far can one endure being alone without the understanding of others."*

Now is our chance to test that theory, to see if we can "form a heart" and "become a responsible, alive self." I quit smoking cold turkey. I quit my relationship cold turkey as well. Quitting my relationship was far worse. It felt a bit like deciding to quit breathing. I seriously thought

I might die from it, because that soupy stew bubbling up in my brain made it feel that way. But I didn't, and you won't either. I promise.

You know that saying, "Time heals all wounds"? Well, I HATE that saying. In the early stages of my breakup, when someone said that to me, I would immediately flash on a mental picture of me stabbing that person with a butter knife. No one UNDERSTOOD! No one could POSSIBLY understand the kind of pain I was experiencing. In some cases, this may have been true. The reason is because, while our friends and family may have certainly experienced heartbreak in their lives, the *immediacy* of the feeling—that crazy *intensity*—has long since faded. Thus, they have only memories, but not a true physical response. This is similar to how mothers can tell you that childbirth was painful, but their bodies don't actually store the memory of that pain. If they did, it is unlikely they would continue the activities that lead to having those babies! Their lack of physical memory is further proof that time *does* diminish the withdrawal symptoms. We can recall that something hurt us deeply, but the recollection *itself* no longer hurts us deeply.

The next question, then, is this:

What in the hell are you supposed to do while you're waiting
for the crazies to pass?

DEPENDING ON THE length of your relationship, your unique circumstances, and whether you have been able to cease all contact with your ex, it is possible that the worst of this phase may last between 90 and 120 days. Beyond that, it may take 1–2 years to clear your system of all residual chemical effects—but these are really very arbitrary numbers. There is a formula we've all heard—an old wives' tale told—about how it will take you half the length of your relationship to recover. I don't believe this for a moment. The real rule is, **there is no rule**! It depends entirely on all the elements involved in your breakup, the tools you have to cope, and various other circumstances combined with your unique personality that make all the difference. It could take you three weeks, three years, or three lifetimes; however, I will say this: Once the initial chemical effects wear off, it seems quite up to *you*. When is it time to say ENOUGH IS ENOUGH? That's for you to decide.

In the meantime, here are some tips that might help you through the worst of it.

DON'T TALK TO HIM!

Seriously. It will only prolong the time it takes to get over him. While you may tell yourself that you can handle it, ask yourself this: *What am I wanting to get out of this communication with him? Do I think I will get it?* If the answer is **No**, then don't do it. If the answer is **Maybe**, then it's **No**, and don't do it. If the answer is **Yes**, well then, why did you break up in the first place?

I do feel that it's important to add the following: It may be the case that there are children involved. This means that it may be impossible for you to cease all contact with your ex-partner. If this is the case, then the recommendation is to keep the contact as limited as possible, and be sure to set very clear boundaries regarding the kinds of contact you have. For example, try to keep interactions short, to the point, and as pleasant (or at least as neutral) as possible while you are going through your healing process. Children can change the dynamic of a breakup to an extreme degree. It can be very tempting, for example, to use the children as a shield, a bludgeon, or even to involve them in what I like to call Ex-S/O Espionage—essentially debriefing them when they return from a visit, demanding that they provide a full report regarding the activities of your ex. This is a thousand times worse than Facebook spying! The results of these behaviors can be disastrous not only for you but for your children as well. In short, *Don't talk to him!* But if you have to, *Keep it brief and focused!*

Don't talk to his friends

I'm sorry. I know this is hard. But it's important for you to identify your triggers, and mutual friends are going to be a BIG one. I learned this the hard way. I thought I might be able to keep some of them—specifically the friends that had been *my* friends apart from him, but then I knew they were still hanging out with James, and the nearly unbearable urge I had to ask about him, find out about him, or relay information to this mutual friend that I thought *might* get back to him was too much to handle. I couldn't do it. I felt miserable. The friendship could no longer be authentic. If this is you, then you may want to go cold turkey on these joint friendships as well. The most important thing right now is for you to take care of *you*.

Eat a healthy diet

Watch out for overuse of stimulants, such as excessive sugar intake, caffeine, and nicotine (which, of course, is probably the exact opposite of what you had in mind). These things combine with the chemicals already released into your system and intensify their effects. Avoid excessive amounts of alcohol. In the case of alcohol, which is a depressant, it may make you feel better at first by masking the symptoms of your pain, but it will eventually drop you lower than your initial low. Instead, try to focus on eating smaller meals more frequently throughout the day. Increase your intake of vegetables. Consider taking a multi-vitamin and drink plenty of water. (Seriously, though, since I know how ridiculous this sounds to the recently afflicted, at least try not to stay too long in the alcohol, ice cream, alcohol, cigarettes, alcohol, pizza, jelly donuts phase.)

Cooking

Cooking can be considered a creative activity—even if we're not master chefs, there is something about the act of cooking that is psychologically beneficial. Not only are we creating something that is (hopefully) going to benefit our bodies but also, in the act of creation, we are providing stimulation of our senses. Chopping, mixing, sautéing; seeing a colorful blend of ingredients; smelling the aroma of the food cooking; tasting what we've created—these things all blend together to provide a rich sensory experience.

Of course, you may be more inclined to dial some numbers and get something delivered. If this is you, you might actually want to consider making a switch, just for the time being, to a more hands-on approach to cooking. Again, it doesn't have to be complicated, and you don't have to start big. How about buying a nice, fragrant rice, like Basmati or Jasmine, and cooking it instead of using Uncle Ben's in a box? Learn to fix chicken or fish. Explore the wide variety of vegetables available at your local market. Better yet, find a local farmer's market and talk to the vendors about how best to prepare the various produce available. Fresh can be wonderful! Organic, even better! There are a number of resources for simple recipes, and the act of cooking can serve as more than just a distraction. It can become a pleasurable activity—one that feeds your body and spirit—if you are willing to change the way you think about your time and the energy you invest in your food.

Exercise

Everyone knows that there are physical benefits to exercise, but there are also very important psychological benefits. Regular exercise will help to improve your mood, reduce stress, increase energy, improve body image, and decrease the symptoms of depression. The session does not have to be overlong or intense in order to achieve benefit. As little as ten minutes of moderate exercise can have a positive benefit—although for chronic or clinical depression, a more intensive and regular course is generally needed.

Aerobic exercise releases endorphins, which are "feel-good" hormones that can leave you feeling calm and optimistic, as well as energized. These endorphins can block feelings of pain and create a kind of euphoria. This euphoria has been compared to the effects one might experience from marijuana. If done on a regular basis, our hormone levels can shift, supplying us with a more regular sense of optimism and calm—something very beneficial for those suffering from depression.

Of course, exercise is wonderful for our bodies as well, and our self-esteem. While it might be the last thing you feel like doing, if you consider the benefits, it's well worth pushing yourself to do. After all, looking absolutely awesome is great revenge, but *feeling* absolutely awesome is typically more useful.

Take walks

This might fall into the category of exercise, but I want to focus here more on the benefits of a soothing walk rather than one undertaken for the purposes of aerobic health. A soothing walk would be one where you are setting off simply to meander and enjoy the outdoors. Taking time out of our busy days to appreciate nature can have great physiological benefit. Slowing down allows the brain a chance to relax. Focusing on beauty brings that beauty to us. Immersing ourselves in the sights, sounds, and smells of nature can be calming and serve to remind us that we are connected to something larger than our own immediate troubles. Nature is one of the best teachers we will ever encounter. It has mastered the one essential element needed for a peaceful life: the ability to let go and change.

BABY YOURSELF

This is critical in the early stages, but it's really important for us to learn at any time in our lives—single or not. Taking the time out to be good to ourselves is critical to our well-being and sense of calm. Remember when you were a baby and something nasty or uncomfortable was taking place? (Okay, you probably don't remember.) Regardless, I'm certain there was a time when you had a wet diaper, or you were hungry, or cold, or you just wanted somebody to come and pick you up and cuddle you in their arms. So you cried, and someone (hopefully!) came and did just that. They *soothed* you.

Well, now is the time when something uncomfortable is taking place. While it's possible that you have wonderful best buddies and family who may be willing to come to your rescue now when you cry, another very crucial skill for you to develop at this time is the ability to self-soothe. This is important because, as adults, it is unlikely that there will *always* be someone there to take care of us when we need for them to do so. As sad as this is, it's the truth. And when this is the case, being able to self-soothe is useful.

This soothing may be different for everyone. The key is to find out what makes you feel the most comfortable and content, even when circumstances are bad. This could be any of the following: a cup of tea or hot chocolate, snuggling beneath a comfy blanket to watch a good movie, reading a book in your favorite chair, gardening, enjoying music, creating art, hiking in the woods, etc. The key is to choose whatever it is that makes you feel calm and relaxed. If you aren't sure what that is, you might try some of the items further down on this list. For me, reading a good novel tucked up beneath a comfy throw is one of my all-time most reliable self-soothing activities.

Also, a word about self-soothing activities vs. destructive ones: the key is moderation. Basically, anything that makes you feel BAD or GUILTY after doing it (like excessive eating, shopping, or drinking) probably doesn't qualify.

CONSIDER A MAKEOVER / FOCUS ON THE BODY

Let's face it. Your breakup probably didn't leave you feeling very confident in the arena of physical appearance. Any type of rejection tends to make us feel bad about ourselves, and it's very easy for this negativity to slip into our sense of body image.

In order to combat this very real side effect, I would recommend focusing on caring for your body to the best of your ability. While this includes exercise and diet, which I've already mentioned, it's also natural to feel like making more superficial changes—new clothes, new hair, new makeup. (Some people really go overboard and start altering body parts.) I think true beauty is one of internal and emotional health, but I will say that anything healthy that can help you feel more confident and loving toward yourself can be beneficial.

After my breakup, I got rid of a lot of my old clothes—especially the ones I'd amassed specifically for the purpose of going to see James perform. Growing up in the music business, I'd learned that appearance can be an important part of a performer's persona, and there was always talk that one day, James and I might play together. I tried to present myself with this in mind, and now those clothes were a reminder that I didn't need to have hanging in my closet. As extreme as it might sound, I got rid of almost everything as a symbol of starting fresh.

I also began a healthier physical routine and, after a while, I started to see an overall improvement in the way that I felt.

ACUPUNCTURE

Acupuncture is the insertion of needles into superficial structures of the body, such as the skin, usually at acupuncture points (meridians). This technique originates from China and has been practiced for thousands of years. The goal is to influence the flow of *qi*, which is loosely translated to mean one's life energy, life force, or energy flow. This is thought to relieve pain and treat or prevent various diseases.

The World Health Organization compiled a list of disorders for which they feel acupuncture may be an appropriate treatment. This includes adverse reactions to radiation treatment, induction of labor, sciatica, dysmenorrhea, depression, hypertension, arthritis, and low back pain.[7] However, practitioners of the art suggest that acupuncture may treat some emotional disorders as well, such as panic attacks, anxiety, post-traumatic stress disorder, depression, phobias, and general stress management.

While the emotional benefits may not be backed by definitive scientific evidence, the one item common to both the lists generated by practitioners and the World Health Organization is *depression*.

Most likely, depression is primary on the list of emotions you are feeling at this time, and you may find some relief in acupuncture. Since this practice is becoming more and more common in our Western culture, it should not be difficult to find someone near you who can provide this service.

ENERGETIC CORD CUTTING OR DISSOLVING

This may be a new one for many of you. The concept here is that whenever we forge new relationships with others, whether they are intimate partnerships, acquaintanceships, or friendships, we are connected to that person by a "cord" of energy and intention. These cords connect us, and through them we transmit information and feelings. The more intense the "connection" we feel with the other individual, the larger that cord becomes, allowing for a greater volume of information and energy transfer. This can be a great source of loving energy exchange, feeding each other very positive input, or it can become a source of very negative energy, where we begin to feel ourselves being drained by these connections.

Perhaps you have heard the term "energy vampirism." This is when it feels like someone close to us is draining us of our life force. We may be giving a lot of ourselves to this person—our time, our love, our support, our money—and yet we feel like we are not getting much back from them. The "cord" between us ceases to be a conduit for an equal energy exchange. It begins to feel like a one-way channel. Worse is the type of connection where we exchange *negative* energy with the other person. The exchange in which we are engaging is filled with a lot of anger, pain, or fear. We are constantly fighting or struggling for a position of power. This all drains us and can lead to depression, exhaustion, low energy, anxiety, and a general sense of being unwell.

Perhaps there was quite a lot of this negative exchange toward the end of your relationship, and now that you are apart, there is a chance that you still feel this drain taking place. I certainly did. Although James was no longer a part of my life in the sense that he was physically present, energetically, I still felt very connected to him. In fact, all of the energy I was putting into thinking about him made it seem like I was STILL feeding him my energy—and at a time when I had very little to spare.

A friend brought to my attention this concept of a cord-cutting ritual, whereby through visualization techniques, you picture this cord as a tangible thing and then sever it. There is quite a bit of information you can discover online regarding this process, or you can search out those able to walk through this ritual with you. There are also some practitioners who feel that rather than "cutting" the cord, we should use visualization techniques to "dissolve" the cord, noting that this may be a better way to sever connections to those with whom we have forged deep bonds that equate to very "thick cords."

When visualizing my connection with James, it felt like a very dark and engorged cable. I recalled our relationship and how much I felt I had dedicated to it. There were very tangible things I had given, but almost from the start, I had also poured a lot of my energy into making it work with someone I loved so much. It was this energy that I was still spilling into that cable—the deep-seated desire to love him and to be loved by him in return.

While I can't tell you that the ritual did much for me, I can say that becoming aware of the concept of this connection did help me to become more cognizant of when I was feeding energy into a line that went absolutely nowhere. Picture a hose where one end is connected to a spigot (you) and the other end is just lying on the grass. You're now pumping water (love, energy, time, resources) from one end out onto the lawn. It's wasteful! You're not getting anything from that except a soupy, muddy mess in your yard. When you feel this happening, picture yourself turning off the spigot.

CLEAN / GET ORGANIZED / GET RID OF BREAKUP REMINDERS / REDECORATE

A breakup has a way of making you want to throw things away. Sometimes, this can be fueled by anger (those tirades where you comb through your house looking for every little thing he ever gave you or that reminds you of him), but it can also be a healthy way to clear out the clutter of a life that no longer suits you.

Personally, I have a basement full of "stuff." I don't know what half the stuff is, and since I haven't used it in all this time, I figure I must not need it. Once a week, I try to fill a single garbage bag with trash and put it out. Over time, the idea is to clear out much of what isn't needed—but don't feel like you have to wait!

Go through your house and get rid of anything you feel you no longer need. Pack it up and deliver it to the Salvation Army or Goodwill. If it's a larger item, such as a piece of furniture, many organizations offer a free pick-up option. This is especially good if there's something you're looking to get rid of that won't fit in your car or is too heavy for you to lift.

On the other side of this is the option to spruce up your house a bit. If you used to live with your ex-partner, now might be the time to redecorate the space and make it your own. This will also help to move you away from visual reminders of your life together.

If change is to be the order of the day, then you might as well embrace it and direct it.

Volunteer

Getting out of the house may be the last thing you want to do right now, which is also what makes it a good idea. Volunteering automatically takes you out of yourself—especially if you choose to volunteer with an organization that helps those who are ill or in need. While volunteering can help connect you to others—increasing your social contacts—it can also help to combat depression. This is not simply because it reduces your sense of isolation; it can also help to remind you that whatever fate you may be experiencing, there are others who are also in need. This doesn't just mean you have to volunteer in a hospital or soup kitchen. You can also volunteer to work with children or even work at a national park.

You can find local volunteer opportunities through community arts organizations, libraries, senior citizen groups, youth organizations, sports teams, animal shelters, church, and online databases. Think of what you're interested in doing and what might fit within your schedule. It doesn't have to be a big commitment—even once a week could provide you with surprising benefits.

JOIN A GROUP

Yes, there is a League of Local Spelunkers or Might and Magic Muffin Night for everyone. Somewhere out there is a group that is perfectly suited to you.

I am a notorious recluse. My job keeps me incredibly busy. Add to that the fact that I don't feel comfortable in a lot of boisterous social situations, but that doesn't mean I don't have any interests! I love to paint, I love to write, and generally I love being around creative types. I was lucky in that I was able to find a group of people who were perfect for me. They combined my love of humor, irreverence, and creative arts in one—forming a community of poets who participate in a weekly show known as Writers' Block Poetry.

Being a part of this group and sharing in our love of expression and humor literally felt like a live-saving connection. Many of the regular members quickly became my friends. Sharing a space with them gave me something to look forward to each week when there was precious little else in my life to smile or laugh about.

There are groups of people meeting up all over the place. In fact, there's even a website called Meetup.com that will help you to connect with all the different events happening in your area. Make sure you investigate each group in order to be safe, but I highly recommend getting involved in something, if you are not already.

GET A HOBBY

If you can't think of something you'd enjoy doing, or that you always wanted to do, that's a problem. You might even consider discussing this with a counselor, as I firmly believe that it's the little things such as these that make life more enjoyable. So…find something you appreciate and latch on to it. (No, drinking wine and eating ice cream don't count!) It also doesn't count if your hobby causes you stress. In my opinion, your hobby should be something that brings you pure bliss—or at least makes you feel very good while you're doing it—and does not have unhealthy side effects.

For me, this involves playing music and painting. I don't have to be a master musician or painter in order to get something immensely fulfilling out of the experience. Anything that can put you into a meditative zone is worth exploring. You could put together wooden boats, garden, learn to knit, do paint by numbers, take up an instrument, learn to ballroom dance—anything. Try something new. You might be surprised by how much less frightening new things are now that your guard is down.

EXPRESSIVE THERAPY

Expressive therapy is defined as the use of art, music, dance, drama, writing, and play in rehabilitation (either emotional or physical). This form of therapy can be done with a guided, trained therapist or in groups, or you can experiment on your own and determine what might work best for you. (In some cases, however, having a guide can enhance the benefits of these therapies.) I've provided a few examples below:

Art therapy – The use of visual media in order to express or identify emotions. This can be completed through painting, collage, drawing, a combination of mixed media elements, and images.

Music therapy – listening to or playing music in order to affect changes in the brain, either emotional changes, physical changes, or to enhance cognitive functioning.

Drama therapy – encourages role-play and acting in order to process emotions or expand one's character.

Dance or movement therapy – uses movement with the acknowledgment that the mind and body are interconnected, thereby using conscious movement in order to unlock and release emotion.

Writing therapy – uses storytelling, poetry, free association, etc., in order to express thoughts and emotions. This can often unlock deep feeling and allow for the release of strong emotions.

TRADITIONAL THERAPY

Never underestimate the benefit of good old-fashioned talk therapy.

You may be one of those people who feels embarrassed by the very notion of going to a therapist, but believe me when I say that the stigma that was once attached to this form of assistance is no longer what it once was (i.e., that going to a therapist means you are crazy). In this modern day, most of the medical profession believes that we should simply throw pills at the things that ail us; however, there are many cases where dealing with our emotional issues may, in fact, help us to deal better with the physical consequences such emotions often engender. If you gave me a choice between taking a pill for the rest of my life and talking over my problems with a trained third-party, I would choose the latter in a heartbeat. The pill may only treat the symptom.

Therapy can come in many forms and from many places. The best thing you can do is carefully research your options. Most therapists will describe, in detail, not only their training but also their methodology. See if it resonates with you. When you choose a therapist, you aren't stuck with that person, either. Find one that suits you—specifically, someone with whom you feel 100 percent comfortable. If you aren't comfortable, move on to the next.

Oftentimes, if you find that you don't have the money to pay for a therapist, you can seek help via a mental health organization or local church. If you are non-denominational, try a Unitarian Universalist church. You may receive a referral to counselors who can work with you within your budget or at no charge for a set number of sessions. There is no reason to be embarrassed. Trust me. Trained therapists have heard it all.

Permit Sadness

Cry! Give yourself permission to feel totally numb and dead and broken and like you will never ever ever love again. Like your heart has been totally crushed, mangled, and it won't beat anymore. There might as well be a petrified log where your heart used to be. It's okay to feel this way. Even when all of your friends and family are telling you that you *shouldn't* be feeling this way, the truth is simple: YOU FEEL THIS WAY. So feel it. And breathe. Breathe. Breathe. Acknowledge it. Say, "This shit sucks. That's okay." From one moment to the next, your feelings will shift. The feelings of grief are like the tide overwhelming you. Your back is to the water, so you never know when that next wave is going to come. I'm not saying that those waves aren't going to knock you around. They are. But some of the tools described here can at least help you to turn around and see them coming. Eventually, you'll even be able to get out of the way, or ride them, or get off the beach and go climb mountains—whatever works for you.

PRACTICE METATHINKING

Metathinking, which may also be referred to as metacognition, is defined as "cognition about cognition" (or "thinking about thinking"). In other words, we are aware of our own thoughts—and hopefully that awareness can lead us to a certain amount of control over them. These thoughts about your thoughts are taking place *while* you are thinking them! In a sense, your brain is looking down upon your brain. You are observing your own process of processing information.

This is an extremely useful tool. When we are able to be aware of the things we're thinking, we are leading ourselves closer to being able to exert some control over our thoughts. It's our thoughts that often lead us into trouble in the first place, and they cause us pain—especially now, since the actual object of our pain may no longer be an active part of our lives. That means every time we experience pain based on something that happened in the past, *we are actually causing ourselves pain by thinking about something unpleasant that is no longer happening in the present.* If we can first become aware of such thoughts, and then move to distance ourselves from them when they occur, we will be on the road to mastering the out-of-control roller coaster of our emotions as well.

Try to observe your thoughts—especially when you notice that you are beginning to feel bad. Go a step further and question those thoughts. Ask yourself, *what does this thought change about my present reality?*

Here's an example: I would often picture James with Sara, then flash back to an argument we'd had near the end when I'd gone into his phone and found a text message from her. When I'd confronted him about the message, he confronted me right back with the violation of his privacy. He was so inflamed about it that I spent the rest of the night and next day apologizing profusely for something that had been grossly out of character for me, all the while realizing that he was deflecting the situation away from the fact that he'd been in regular contact with his ex without my knowledge. Re-envisioning this scenario in the present, knowing that he was now with her and that I'd had cause to be concerned, made my blood burn! *He betrayed me!* I would think, over and over. *He wanted to be with her all along!*

Naturally, these thoughts made me feel bad. When I could catch myself thinking them, I would ask myself, *what do these thoughts change about my present reality?* The answer was almost always the same: Nothing (aside from the fact that they made me feel bad). My reality was unchanged. I was still in the middle of walking down the stairs, for instance, or cooking breakfast, or watching TV, or staring at the ceiling. I might have been snuggled down in my bathrobe, sipping tea, cozy on my couch, safe and warm—yet my thoughts were doing the equivalent of putting me out on the street in the middle of a blizzard, naked, surrounded by a pack of starving wolves. James had hurt me. True. But that was past. *The person hurting me now was me.*

WRITE HIM LETTERS

But DON'T SEND THEM to him!

You might find yourself with an awful lot to say to this person. Some of it may be good and some of it may be incredibly awful. Indeed, this was the case for me. Early on, especially while I was dealing with the overwhelming urge to contact him, I found myself writing James letters. In them, I would tell him how much I missed him, or how sorry I was that it didn't work out. I told him how much I loved him and how I wished the best for him.

Later, I wrote him letters telling him what an asshole he was, and asking him how he could have treated me so poorly when all I'd tried to do was love him to the best of my ability.

Sending him either version of these letters would not have done any good. The first might have made him feel better, of course (which was strong incentive for me to send them, since I'd always wanted him to feel good), but I recognized that there was no way I could send them off without wanting something back. And since I knew that I wasn't going to get back what I wanted, I would only be hurting myself by sending them. Thus, leave such letters in your drawer, or in a file on your computer, as the case may be. If you *really* feel the need to send them off into the world, send them to a trusted friend. Allow them to bear witness to and acknowledge your pain.

WRITE IN A JOURNAL

Writing in a journal can be incredibly healing. This is the repository for all of your dreaming, your fury, your love, your pain, your sorrow—anything and everything. While at first it might just seem like a place where you can take your ranting, the act of expression can actually help to release some of the strong emotions. In addition, you might find that you surprise yourself with the things that come out. It's a great way to learn about yourself. Don't worry about how it sounds. Just write whatever is in your heart.

BE REALISTIC ABOUT THE RELATIONSHIP

That means no more "relationship revisionism." You may need to acquire the help of others at first, since it will be *very* difficult for you to be realistic (especially when the chemicals are rushing through you, insisting that you try to win him back at any cost because he is so absolutely awesome). There were many times when I needed to call up friends who knew me and the details of my relationship. I would ask these friends point-blank to remind me of the things that were *negative* in my relationship. They were often happy to oblige.

Remember, if it had been a perfect relationship, you'd still be in it. Hell, if it had been a *good* relationship, you'd still be in it. But something was wrong with it. Know how I know? You're not in it anymore.

Think about every bad thing he did. Go ahead. It's okay. You have to fight the irrational chemical withdrawal urges with as much rational thinking as possible. This means reminding yourself of the unpleasant aspects of your relationship.

Conversely, stop making singledom out to be like a dreaded plague from which you are likely to die, all crusted over and wasted because no one wants you now and forevermoreamen.

SET SHORT-TERM GOALS

These can be daily goals—*today, I will shower and get dressed; today, I will work late and get the job done; today, I will tackle laundry*—or they can be slightly further-reaching: *I will begin going out and being social after one month of sitting on my couch in furry penguin pajama pants, watching every episode of* Star Trek: The Next Generation *currently streaming on Netflix.*

SET LONG-TERM GOALS

Now is a great time to decide what you want for your life. Things have just pretty much collapsed around you, so what better time than now to build something new? Think of all the things that you may have wanted to do but didn't have time to do before. Was your relationship holding you back in any way? Was it tying you down to a particular location? Were there things you wanted to try that you simply never got around to?

Well, here is your chance.

If you have trouble thinking of something, try a visual exercise: Go out and buy a bunch of magazines (or go to the library and peruse their collection; used bookstores might also have really cheap old magazines). Go through and look at the pictures. See what calls to you. Does it bring anything to mind that you'd like to try or that *resonates* with you?

PRACTICE GRATITUDE

This may take a while. At first, you won't be grateful for anything. That's okay. Journal about the stuff that's NOT FAIR. There's plenty of material there. Eventually, as the chemicals wear off, you will find little things here and there that make you feel good again. When you notice them, just stop for a moment to acknowledge them. Out loud. The same as you acknowledge the bad things. Just say something like, "I had a really nice time on my walk today." Your heart will be raw, so you may be more open to noticing other people. Sometimes, a kind word or wave might set you on the way to feeling grateful. For me, there were dozens of little things like this: my neighbor mowing my lawn for me or taking my trashcan to the curb; the way he watched over me if someone strange came to the door or stopped me when I was outside; the fatherly salesman at Lowe's helping me pick out a showerhead; friends checking in on me when they knew I'd been feeling low. Even in the midst of our pain, there are still little glimmers of light.

Forgiveness Work

Eventually, you're going to have to do it. You are going to have to forgive not only him but also yourself. You did everything that you could do, and it still didn't work out. He was perfectly himself, and it still didn't work out. It's okay. You are both imperfectly perfect beings, and everything that happened was perfect just the way it was. That doesn't mean you are going to feel GOOD about it yet. That may take years, if ever. But at the least, it's important for you to realize that everyone did the best they could with what they had and who they are at this point in time. That includes you. That includes him.

There were many nights I sat up, just like I did when we were first getting together, pressing my palm to the back of my couch as if I were reaching out and pressing it against his chest, right where his heart was. Then, I would pray to the universe to take care of him, to watch over him. His life was difficult, and I wanted the chance to be a part of it to make it better. (Arrogant, but I had good intentions.) Finally, there I was again, pressing my palm to the back of the couch as if touching his heart, but this time, I said, "I'm so sorry I could not give you what you needed. I'm so sorry it did not work out." I prayed to the universe to take care of him and to watch out for him. In the beginning, I told myself that I would always want what was best for him, *even if that was not me.* The universe, it seemed, was going to hold me to that.

THE MAJORITY OF books that discuss Buddhist principles are going to rely heavily on one daily practice: meditation. In most cases, what comes to mind when people hear this word is "sitting meditation." For instance, in Zen Buddhism, zazen is the practice of "seated meditation" performed in order to calm the mind and body. Zazen is done in order to help you suspend thinking and let words, ideas, thoughts, and judgments pass without getting involved in them. Contrary to some beliefs, the idea is not to stop thinking. Just you try to do that! It's like trying to grip water in your fist. No matter how tightly you hold, it keeps creeping through the cracks until all the water is gone. You may not be able to stop thinking, but you *can* let the thoughts come and go without getting yourself wrapped up in them. In some cases, you can breathe in and out, count your breaths, label your thoughts "thinking," and then return to the breath.

When we think meditation, we also think of a specific posture, usually sitting on the floor or on cushions, mats, or benches, folded legs and hands, an erect but settled spine, breathing from the center of the belly, eyelids half lowered (not closed). But meditation can also be thought of as follows: "any form of a family of practices in which practitioners train their minds or self-induce a mode of consciousness to realize some benefit."[8]

Another way of looking at the practice of mediation is to consider it as "witnessing." We are witnessing our minds in action (metacognition). See how wonderful (terribly ridiculous!) they are? And guess what? You don't have to be seated, hands folded, in order for this to take place. Because meditation can be considered witnessing, or having awareness, there are a number of ways that we can do this beyond the traditional approach. I will delve into this later, but for now, suffice to say that becoming witness to your own mind can, at first, be alarming.

Here's the thing: Meditation is wonderful. Sitting meditation is not for everyone. I say that as one who has tried it numerous times over the years (normally when there is something dreadful happening in my life, and I'd really like to shut up my brain). Why do I keep trying? Because the benefits are *well* documented.

In a study published online in the April 21 journal *Brain Research Bulletin*,[9] researchers found that people trained to meditate over an eight-week period were better able to control their alpha rhythms. Alpha waves flow through the cells in the brain's cortex where sensory information is processed. These waves help suppress irrelevant or distracting sensory information. Having greater control over these alpha waves allows meditators to "turn down the volume" on certain signals, including those related to pain. There is also a marked reduction in stress. Deep breathing increases the circulation of oxygen to the muscles. Meditation can also lower high blood cholesterol, strengthen the immune system, increase emotional self-control (decreasing reactivity), provide a greater enjoyment of subtleties through increased awareness, increase mental focus and clarity, and provide greater self-awareness, leading to an increased sense of connectedness. Additional studies have shown that meditation can also serve to reduce feelings of loneliness

In short, it can help you feel happier, calmer, and more accepting in your daily life. Awesome, right?

But sitting? Sitting and watching the brain?

Yeah, awful.

First of all, if you're like most people who have led a sedentary lifestyle, or you have a work schedule that requires you to sit at a computer for long periods of time, or you suffer from health problems (or simply have terrible posture), then the process of sitting can actually be very uncomfortable, even downright painful. I certainly fall into this category. Sitting for me often made it difficult to breathe, as my body posture and shallow breathing habits combined to make a change in this department one my body rebelled against quite loudly. Feeling out of breath is very common. Of course, you can train yourself over time to sit with the pain, and this is a good practice. It is worth pursuing. But I tell you this: When you are drowning in grief, and your mind is spinning a mile a minute, and you want to cry every second, and you don't know whether you can make it another instant, sitting in meditation barely able to breathe with your body crying out in pain might not work for you. In this case, you're likely to abandon the process and not get any of the benefits described above, which would be tragic. (On the other hand, it might work very well, since the pain in your body might distract you from the pain in your heart.)

In addition to this, I feel it's a MUST for me to note that the majority of Buddhist-centric relationship advice out there today relies heavily on mediation as a way to make it through. I say, if you're already reasonably physically healthy, or you are already familiar with the practice, then yes. Yes! But if you're new to it, or have had trouble with it in the past, this advice may feel frustrating. Yes, I know I should meditate. And yes, it's helpful. And yes, I want to do it. But I have Failed Miserably each time, and it just adds to my frustration. So does that mean it's hopeless?

No!

Not when we consider the fact that one aspect of what we're going for is mind training. If part of meditation is about awareness, about being a witness to our thinking and learning to stay in the present moment, then there are countless other ways we can do this to *start* us along the path to greater self-awareness, which will fit into our busy lifestyle and provide us with benefits no matter what. I am not saying that these methods will bring about sudden enlightenment. I feel that sitting meditation and actually dealing with all of the uncomfortable and painful things that arise from the practice are _very important_ to the process of becoming a more evolved person; however, we're talking about getting through a breakup here—not necessarily achieving complete spiritual enlightenment!

That said, mind training is no joke, seated or not. It is still difficult. Becoming aware of the present moment may sound easy, but when you really stop and do it, you will realize that we are very, very seldom *in the moment*.

I have a ritual every morning that involves doing my dishes by hand. Yes, by hand. I have a perfectly fine dishwasher, and I still choose to do my own dishes by hand. For one, I am the only one for whom I am cooking at the moment, so I really don't generate a great many dishes in a day. Two, this is a great way to fill time in the morning. For me, morning was one of the worst periods to get through in the beginning. I would wake up and the whole miserable scene would come flooding back. Open eyes? *Check.* Sleeping on the couch again? *Check.* All alone? *Check.* Did the man I love really just drive to another state to be with his ex-girlfriend, cuddle up to her, and then pose for a picture that she would post to her Facebook profile? *Check.*

So imagine me standing in front of the sink, struggling to get my day going. There is a sink full of dirty dishes in front of me, and this is a perfect chance to be in the moment. Normally, such a task as boring as dishwashing would be below our level of attention. It is mundane, and it allows quite a lot of space to let our minds wander. But wander to what? In my case, my mind would wander in all sorts of unpleasant directions—namely, Facebook photos; so instead, I tried to pay attention to what I was doing. "Washing a butter knife," I might say to myself, or "scrubbing a bowl." Naturally, the next moment, I would become aware that underneath my attention on scrubbing various things was a steady chatter. For instance, a popular Top 40 song called "Breakeven" by The Scripts was beaming the following lines directly into my head, monotonously: "One still in love while the other one's leaving/Cause when a heart breaks, no it don't breakeven"…the same lines over and over and over. On top of that were thoughts about how senseless it was to have a single line of a song repeating itself over and over, and isn't it weird to be aware of it all of a sudden, and that makes me feel a little crazy, and now I'm washing a fork, and it used to be that James' dog would circle around my feet waiting for me to drop food but now there's only my cat waiting for me to feed him canned cat food, and hearts certainly DON'T break even, that's a fact, and I'm washing a plate now that had cat food on it, and the cat is flopping himself over my feet trying to get my attention, and James always hated the smell of cat food…

So on and so forth. You see how it takes quite a bit of practice to be in the moment, even just to wash a fork, or a plate?

There were also those mornings when I would call my mother while I was washing dishes and then moving on to the task of cooking breakfast. These mornings were the most telling of all. As I grew used to at least *attempting* to focus on the task at hand, I found that those mornings when I would talk with her, and my body just automatically completed all the tasks I put before it, I couldn't help but feel like I'd forgotten something, or like I'd done something incorrectly because I hadn't been focused on it. I found that there were some mornings when breakfast would just appear before me, completely cooked, and I realized that I hadn't been present for the making of it—not mentally. As time passed, I came to dislike that feeling.

Being present comes with its own reward. At some point, you come to realize that all of the things that so often bring us pain are events that *are not actually happening*. They may have happened in the past, but they are not happening *now*. We simply relive them over and over and blow them up into stories that live on in us. It's as if we've been in a major car wreck that we didn't see coming, and so in an effort to understand what happened, we go out driving every day, re-creating the accident from every angle we can imagine. And every day, we're injured in our search for some ultimate meaning. If we can be in the moment, even for a little while, then we can stop the behaviors that escalate our pain—the ones taking place in our heads.

TOP 10 BILLBOARD Charts after the breakup.

Oct. 22, 2011

1. Someone Like You (Adele)
2. Moves Like Jagger (Maroon 5 ft. Christina Aguilera)
3. Pumped Up Kicks (Foster the People)
4. Sexy and I Know It (LMFAO)
5. Stereo Hearts (Gym Class Heroes ft. Adam Levine)
6. Party Rock Anthem (LMFAO ft. Lauren Bennett & Goonrock)
7. We Found Love (Rihanna ft. Calvin Harris)
8. Without You (David Guetta ft. Usher)
9. You Make Me Feel (Cobra Starship ft. Sabi)
10. You and I (Lady Gaga)

Honorable mentions:

"Rolling in the Deep" (Adele), which played nearly non-stop for the next five months—a torturous anthem for the broken-hearted if ever there was one. (P.S. Hearing this song made me want to plug my ears with corroded batteries.)

"Somebody That I Used to Know" (Gotye). If my breakup had a theme song, this would have been it.

This is the soundtrack that accompanied me on all my rides *everywhere*. Outside my window, I saw a steady stream of college kids going about their gloriously young lives. Inside my car, I heard a steady stream of music that brought about deep feelings of despair. Changing the channel never seemed to help. I never quite knew what the trigger would be.

The emotional response we have to music is different for everyone, having largely to do with the associations we have made over time. For me, God forbid a station should play "Werewolves of London," or far worse, that one time in Big Lots where they began to pipe in, "You and I" by Wilco—a song I'd once put on a "mix-CD" for James. It was either abandon my cart of sundries and flee the store or continue shopping with tears rolling down my cheeks. (I chose the latter.)

You might begin to feel as if every song on the radio is either mocking you or pushing you to drive your car over a cliff. Contrary to how you might feel in those moments, music *can* be a wonderful tool for healing. You just have to figure out how to use it.

Studies have found that music has a very definite impact on the brain, including a causal relationship between music and the motivation and reward system. This is the system we discussed in the chapter that dealt with the science of falling in love. Listening to music *that is pleasurable* triggers the release of dopamine during moments of peak emotional arousal. You may have found yourself getting "chills" when you listened to a certain piece of music, or a certain part of a song may give you a little "rush" of pleasure. That is part of the dopamine response, and as you should now be aware, this dopamine is what we are craving most intensely after the withdrawal of our partner (who used to be a trigger for dopamine).

The stress here, however, is on *pleasurable* music. If you find yourself listening to the mix-CD he made you, filled with songs that trigger memories of your love, you may find yourself flooded with sorrowful feelings instead, which often enhance the craving for what we have lost. While unlocking tears can help us to release strong emotion, or the music can serve as a surrogate, seeming to release that emotion for us, it may not bring about the pleasant feelings for which we are hoping—and it is possible to push ourselves deeper into depression.

Music that makes us feel good or uplifted can have many other positive benefits. It can help us to lower the perception of effort during exercise or other mundane tasks, increase energy efficiency, reduce anxiety and stress, help to lower heart rate and blood pressure, and relieve pain (or our perception of pain). If we can focus on sound, it may also help to keep us in the present moment, which can be a great benefit when our current condition is one of past-centered focus, reliving our recent experience. A present-centered outlook can increase feelings of calm and contentment.

In addition, sound vibrations can be healing. Music that has a narrow pitch range or soft, predictable, and possibly triple meter rhythms (mimicking a rocking motion) can have a soothing effect, impacting our heart rate and respiration.

Rhythmic Entrainment and Biomusicology

"Biomusicology," a term first introduced by Nils L. Wallin in 1991,[11] is the study of music from a biological point of view.

"Entrainment," as related to biomusicology, refers to the synchronization of organisms to an external rhythm.[12] A simple example of this would be tapping your foot or clapping your hands to the sound of a beat.

Rhythmic entrainment can occur when two vibrating bodies come into contact with each other. This entrainment can be seen in many examples throughout nature, but it can also be demonstrated in mechanical objects. For instance, if you were to place two or more mechanical metronomes on a moveable plank, then set each metronome's needle to a different starting position, eventually the metronomes would come into phase.

It takes less energy to work in coordination than in opposition. Nature loves efficiency! Picture a rowing crew, with all the rowers working together, in rhythm, versus each one stroking his or her oars randomly. Working "in concert" equals greater progress than working against each other. This is a social function that serves mankind very well in terms of survival, and it may be one of the reasons why humans have developed such a strong ability to synchronize with external rhythms.

One of the reasons why my daily sojourns out into the world, driving along to the radio "soundtrack of despair," often left me feeling more depressed than ever was that I was connecting with that specific music in a way that led me deeper *into* depressed thoughts and feelings. The musical selections most often on the radio held associations for me that left me feeling sad, and there was no resultant change in the tone that led me to a more positive feeling.

The reverse side of this is that simply forcing ourselves to listen to "upbeat" and "positive" music when we are in a depressed state *feels wrong*. It doesn't match the mood we're in, so there is something about it that feels false, and we find ourselves unable to *connect* (entrain).

When we talk about music entrainment, as it might relate to music therapy, the exercise I have found to be most successful in the alteration of depressed states is one described in detail by John M. Ortiz, Ph.D. in his book *The Tao of Music: Using Music to Change Your Life*. In the Appendix section that deals with entrainment, Ortiz describes the principles behind using specific music selections to change our mental state.

The key to inflicting the changes we seek may be a concept known as *isomorphism*. In biology, isomorphism is the similarity of form or structure between organisms. In psychology (specifically Gestalt psychology), it is a correspondence between a stimulus and the brain state created by that stimulus. In our case, the trick here is to use the stimulus of music to first *match* our current brain state before we try to *change* that brain state. We want to *guide* ourselves slowly to the emotional state in which we wish to be rather than force ourselves into a sudden change.

John Ortiz (*The Tao of Music*) recommends the use of an "Entrainment Tape" in order to accomplish this. While the term itself might be a bit outdated—since very few of us are still recording music on cassette tapes—the heart of the practice is still very relevant and useful. The basic exercise includes creating a uniquely personal playlist of music that will take you on a journey. The first step would be to choose music *that matches your current mood*.

In creating my own list, in order to deal with my frequent deep depression over my breakup with James, I first chose a few songs that quite adequately reflected my emotional state over the breakup. These were songs that reminded me heavily of James and made me feel very sad and nostalgic. (Yes, including the Wilco "theme song" that nearly chased me out of Big Lots.)

Then I continued on, adding several musical selections that were moderately less sad and upsetting—somewhere in between the emotional state I was currently experiencing and the state where I wanted to be.

Finally, I began adding music that better reflected the mood I wanted—a state of calm, perhaps. I chose music that brought about feelings of acceptance, equanimity, even pleasure and optimism for the future.

Here is my personal "Recovery" playlist:

"From the Morning" – Nick Drake
"You and I" – Wilco
"Kite Song" – Pattie Griffin
"Either Way" – Wilco
"More Than This" – Charlie Hunter, Featuring Norah Jones
"Cold Water" – Damien Rice
"Gravity" – Sara Bareillas
"After the Tears" – Jonatha Brooke
"Slowly, Surely" – Jill Scott
"Details in the Fabric" – Jason Mraz
"Keep Breathing" – Ingrid Michaelson
"Bruised But Not Broken" – Joss Stone
"The Heart of the Matter" – India Arie (Don Henley, orig.)
"I Was Brought to My Senses" – Sting
"Count Me In" – Early Winters
"Beautiful Day" – U2
"Golden" – Jill Scott
BONUS "Beyond" – L. Subramanium

It took me around two hours to put together this list. I tried to approach it as I would the telling of a story. I started out with a piece of music that I'd very positively and concretely associated with the falling in love phase of my relationship. (I chose well. The first time I listened to this list, I burst into tears within the first thirty seconds of the first song!) The remainder of the list progressed deeper in to the relationship, where I began to feel a lot of sadness and uncertainty. It then progressed to the actual breakup and on, through the recovery phase to the point where I *wanted* to be: which was to feel very upbeat and hopeful about the future. My list was a bit long, coming in (before the bonus track) at a little over an hour. I made an event of listening to it for the first time, dimming the lights and settling in with no distractions. I even used headphones so that I could be completely immersed in the music. By the time I was finished, I felt cleaned out.

The bonus track was an add-on I decided upon at the last minute. This one track, which is a beautiful piece of Indian Classical music, is 28 minutes long and entirely instrumental. This single piece of music had the ability to take me on a journey all on its own, without words.

Keep in mind, your list will look very different from mine—and it's fine if you create one that is shorter or longer. It might be beneficial, in fact, to have two lists: a long one and then one that is more condensed. Overall, the most important thing to keep in mind is that this only works if you choose music that SPECIFICALLY evokes the feelings you are attempting to emphasize and then finally create for yourself. That might mean digging out the music you'd previously banned because it made you think of him (all that Wilco and Nick Drake, in my case). This playlist should be uniquely your own and can include any genre of music you like, with lyrics or without. No two playlists will be alike. The more time and thought you put into this, the greater your results will be. You might also find that you put together an initial list, listen to it, note the tracks that have the greatest impact (and the ones that suddenly feel out of place), and amend your playlist to maximize its impact. I also found that as time passed, I could start the playlist at about the mid-way point to match my overall improving mood, rather than having to start at the beginning with the more emotionally charged music. (Today, I could listen to this entire playlist and only feel nostalgic and benevolent.)

I had a lot of success with this approach. I also branched out and created additional playlists, which were designed to augment other activities. For instance, I created a playlist filled with energetic music for when I wanted to get things accomplished or inspire myself to dance or exercise. A playlist filled with angry music worked great for getting up and letting myself just move around and work out all that aggressive energy.

Music streaming stations such as Pandora, Spotify, etc., can also be a great aid, since you can customize your playlists based on artists or genres. This will introduce you to a lot of new music. I frequently used the "Bookmark" function on Pandora to save songs that I particularly liked, or that evoked a specific emotional response, and then later I would purchase that single track as an MP3 from Amazon and add it to a playlist.

Once you have your customized playlists, carry them with you. I loaded mine onto my cell phone. This allowed me to have it available wherever I was. When I was out driving, rather than listen to the radio, I would put on one of my playlists. In the morning—one of the worst times for me—I would put on a "wake up" list while doing the dishes. Eventually, I found myself listening to one of my playlists while doing almost *everything* where there would otherwise have been nothing but a bunch of silence (which I would have been inclined to fill with a non-stop jumble of bitter, angry, and depressing thoughts). I even put a small set of speakers in my bathroom so that I could play music while I was taking a shower!

I want to add a note here that you can also choose to pick up an instrument and create music yourself; however, if you are not a musician, there is the possibility that you might find it more challenging to create an altered state for yourself using this method. You may find it easy to play something that entrains with your current mood; however, if your skillset with the instrument you are playing is limited, you may find yourself having trouble moving to a state with your music that will bring you to a new place of calm. If this is the case, then you may want to stick with choosing music that's already been created. But I *will* say here that I have had great success in playing music with a group of people that led to enhanced states of consciousness. Entraining with a *group* of people can be a very powerful and uplifting experience. Even if you're not well-trained, sometimes something as simple as picking up a drum and finding a local drum circle can do wonders for uplifting your spirit (and it has the added benefit of being social).

Regardless of the exact method or music we choose, we should be aware that we can consciously take part in re-programming ourselves by exploiting one of our most basic instincts, which is to *work in synch*.

For me, such exercises also helped bring me *into the moment* (where no one was actively engaged in hurting me), but naturally there were limitations.

I couldn't, for instance, create a playlist that would cure me of my increasingly obsessive need to examine every Red Minivan that passed me on the road.

And they were EVERYWHERE.

THE ROAD WAS thick with possession. High Street. North Broadway. State Route 161 or 315. Olentangy River Road. Left lane. There! Dodge Grand Caravan. Ford Freestar. Toyota Sienna. Chevy Venture. The make and model were elusive—I simply couldn't recall what it was—only that it was a red minivan (the shade of which was a perfect match to my own Toyota), and the license plate number corresponded with my birth year.

So quite naturally, I saw them everywhere. I mean *every*where. My head would whiplash. I'd crane my neck, turn about, peer at plates. That van coming toward me, moving away, parked in some parking lot—was it *his?* Was it? I peeked into windows as we passed each other. Old ladies. Old men. Young women. Families. It was never him.

He had disappeared from the face of the earth, and when you are used to seeing or talking with someone nearly every single day of your life for close to four years, the sudden absence of that person is jarring, to say the least. You want to catch a glimpse (but you also know it would be awful, so it's all very weird and uncomfortable).

This is another way that stalkers are born. Most likely, I could have driven my car past any one of his old hangout spots after 10PM and identified, once and for all, what the actual make and model was of his stupid red minivan, which had become such an obsession (as if I didn't know where he was living, for that matter—at least in the beginning). Yet, I did not drive to any of those places. Not once. I was more terrified of accidently seeing him with another woman than I was of easing my mind by placing a mental pushpin on a map marking his location. Nor did I want to discover that he'd left his current place of residence—and town altogether—in order to move in with his latest girlfriend (which turned out to be the case). Some things—I'd learned the very, very hard way—are better left unknown.

Still, none of this knowledge stopped me from nearly wrecking my car at the sight of red minivans. I even went out of town and *still* found myself checking license plates. I'd have a reaction if I saw a red minivan *in a television program!* (It took about a year for this obsessive-compulsive behavior to work itself out of my body chemistry.) There was simply a part of me that wanted to see him, that wanted to identify that he was still alive. After all, there is a person out there, somewhere, whom I'd once loved with all my heart. The last time I saw him, he was walking out the door telling me, "I'll probably end up in jail somewhere." To which I'd numbly responded, "No you won't. You'll end up married."

I told him I would talk with him again, when a little bit of time had passed. I had no idea that a "little bit of time" would turn into so long or possibly never. I had no idea that the pain I was feeling in that moment would only grow worse. I did not know that he would move on so quickly, and that in doing so, I would not be able to be his friend. I'd always intended to be his friend. How could I not? I loved him. I would *always* love him on some level. That kind of love doesn't just go away. Ever. And yet…

Self-preservation meant that I could not move forward without letting him go so utterly and completely that it meant pulling out bits of myself along with it. I had to open my hand and release every ounce of him. Exhale every breath of him that existed within my body. And this process takes a very long time. Such finality, for me, could only exist with an absolute blackout of contact. A moment of weakness would mean starting again from scratch, and I simply did not have the strength. Also, my pride would not allow it. My pride was the engine behind the effort of an immense anti-backsliding campaign: no phoning, texting, emailing, letters, and above all…*no stalking*.

Turnabout is also fair play. In as much as he had disappeared from me, I had also disappeared from him. What I gave to him had been retracted all the way, an energy beam that had been cut off completely and abruptly. Why must this be so? There are plenty of people who have successfully broken off relationships and remained friends with no pause in between. If you are one of these (ex) couples, hurray! I am happy for you both. One of my very dearest friends just so happens to be an ex-boyfriend. But this might not work with all cases, and if you are like I am, and this particular ex-partner is your kryptonite, then you must stay clear until you are cured of all this craziness or risk losing your super powers.

In my relationship, so much of my energy had been devoted to our maintenance that I did not have much left in reserve for myself. To be sending it off to him after the fact, when I was below zero, was out of the question. I would need every ounce of it for recovery, and this meant

NO CONTACT.

But I had no control over the number of red minivans on the road. There was no way for me to notify the Bureau of Motor Vehicles that my relationship had just suffered the equivalent of a vehicular homicide, and his license should, therefore, be revoked. So he was still out there, steering the giant wheel like the helm of a ship, exploring new worlds, boldly going where no minivan has gone before, passenger seat reserved for his dog, or guitar, or someone else—one medium-red-pearl four-wheeled reminder that he was gone.

The truth is, sooner or later, were I finally to find the one that belongs to him, it would still end up in my rear view mirror, or turning left where I am going right, or stopping when I am moving forward. Two ships passing. That is what we are now. No matter how many of them I see in a day, this fact still remains: I must keep driving.

But maybe not alone.

Enter, the dog.

CHAPTER 8
DEFROSTING YOUR HEART:
KIBBLE AND BITCH

JAMES HAD A dog. I took care of him quite a lot while James was away, but I was never able to bond with him. This was because he was neurotic. It was also because I realized we had something in common. We were being treated in much the same way, which is to say that James treated me much like he treated his dog. He was neglectful; he came and went as he pleased without regard to my own needs, only patting me on the head on his way out and back in. Occasionally, we might go for a walk, or I might otherwise receive some treat from him (possibly a bone).

In return, I waited faithfully by the door listening intently for the sound of his car, which would mark his return. The dog and I would get equally excited. In the end, I knew that if this kept up, I would become as neurotic as the dog. I'd develop nervous ticks and lick the carpet incessantly out of boredom. Whine. Gnaw away patches of skin.

Truthfully, he loved the dog better than he loved me. I was the interloper. Even the dog knew this, and I resented him (the dog, I mean). I resented our commonality. The sun rose and set, for both of us, on the same human who didn't quite deserve it.

Thus, when people began suggesting that I get a dog, I was reluctant. "It's so much more trouble than a cat," I would say. Plus, I had never been so vain that I required the sort of undying affection and devotion people seemed to need from their dogs.

"You are god to a dog," my friend told me. "The opener of all doors."

Who needs that kind of power trip? Cats seemed more honest. They come to you on their own terms—mainly to get food or affection from you, and then they walk away. There aren't any illusions of grandeur you can get from that relationship.

But then I went to visit with my mother for a week. She had a Miniature Pinscher named Tonka, a perfectly ridiculous dog. Its little legs looked like toothpicks, and as is typical of a dog so small that a stiff breeze could knock it down, it had an attitude the size of a Mack truck. It yapped. It raced around in hyper circles. It wore ridiculous sweaters because it didn't seem to have enough fur to keep itself warm. In short, all the things I find annoying about small dogs were present in this one. And yet, at night, it would leap up onto the recliner with me and curl into my arms. It gave love. Its warm little body pressed against my heart, and I felt a thaw.

So, when the subject came up again, I decided to take the plunge. I would get a dog of my own…

Simon came to me at Christmas time. He'd been at the Humane Society for six months and was already a year old. It was his soulful eyes that grabbed me. He was brindle, possibly containing a mixture of Pit Bull, Bulldog, and Labrador—his legs were short, but he was stocky and built. He had the temperament of a Lab, though, and I thought he was sweet.

Before I adopted him, I had him checked out by a vet. He got a clean bill of health, and one morning, I was suddenly a proud dog mommy.

Only it was immediately clear that this was going to take some getting used to. For one, someone had given him a bath, and from the smell of it, they'd bathed him in a barrel of perfume. Given that the slightest hint of artificial fragrance can send me running for the outdoors, the fact that my dog smelled like a perfume counter at Macy's (assuming someone had smashed open every bottle and left the liquids to mingle in the aisle) was a big problem. While he was anxiously wandering about his new environment and trying to figure out who the hell I was, I was trying to breathe.

"Good boy," I said, patting him awkwardly, fingertips plugging my nose.

Also, unfortunately, he had just had surgery to get neutered, so that meant he couldn't have a bath for ten days.

"Ten days!" I told the vet, whom I'd telephoned in desperation. "I can't last ten more seconds!"

They recommended that I try dry shampoo or fragrance free bath wipes to eliminate the odor, so off I raced to the pet store—Simon in tow, since I didn't know him well enough to leave him alone with my cat, and I thought it might be mean to crate him so soon in a strange house. Windows down in 30-degree weather, I tried mouth breathing for the duration of the trip.

The pet store had fragrance-free wipes, and after we got home, it took nearly half the container before I could finally breathe a little easier.

"Good boy," I said again.

He looked at me distrustfully. After all, I'd just spent twenty minutes furiously scrubbing him down with little wet wipes. Not the best way to start our relationship.

Problem 2

That's when the diarrhea started. Like a new mom, I was up every two hours letting him outside, where I watched in horror as he painted the yard. I began cooking him rice and chicken broth twice a day. I'd barely even been cooking for myself! Then there was the pumpkin, because I'd been told that pumpkin helps with diarrhea. My dishes doubled. I was suddenly dedicating a lot of time to the positive state of his bowel movements.

Problem 3

Two different vets over a period of two months gave him no fewer than ten different medications—one for every kind of worm imaginable and a bacteria that, evidently, foments in mud.

"He could have gotten it from your yard," the vet told me.

I was dismayed. It was raining nearly every day. My yard was nothing *but* mud. Was my yard making my dog sick? More pills, and a forty-dollar probiotic to be sprinkled onto his food. More opportunities to traumatize my dog as I tried everything possible to get him to take pills, and a terrible smelling thick liquid in a syringe, which was to be shot directly into the back of his mouth. Have you ever tried shooting something into the back of a dog's mouth when that dog weighs half as much as you do, is all muscle, has a lot of sharp teeth at his disposal, and backs away from you whenever you take hold of him? This was fun. Having a dog = fun.

The shove-syringe-near-sharp-teeth method was a no-go, so enter cans of cat food, which solved the medicine-dispensing problem but worsened the diarrhea. His flatulence was near constant. He would follow me from room to room, christening the air with an odor so foul it would sting my eyes and bring to mind images of rotting broccoli and cauliflower liquefying in vegetable crispers.

"Go away!" I'd say, feeling cross and guilty and desperate all in one.

How could I possibly bond with an animal that pooped pudding, farted more horrifically than someone suffering from the aftereffects of a ten-bean-chili-with-bacon pizza, and who had also quite completely drained my bank account?

Once more to the vet—a new one this time. He told me it wasn't the mud. Thank God! My dog finally tested free of parasites, so we discussed another dog food change. Meanwhile, Simon politely sniffed about the examination room, tooting his butt horn all the while.

Problem 4

I am a bad person.

"What if I don't love my dog yet?" I typed into ask.metafilter.com. Other people appear to fall in love at first sight. They sleep with their dogs, cuddling up with them beneath the covers, sharing a pillow. I, on the other hand, had simply bought my dog four different dog beds (a big and small one for both upstairs and downstairs; he liked to switch back and forth between the two sizes). But why would I want to sleep with him? I still slept on the couch. There just wasn't room. And let's not forget about the farting, shall we?

"You should take him back to the pound if you don't love him," my mother told me, disgusted. I mean, here was a perfectly fine dog—other than his bowel issues. He was polite, well-behaved, and a fast learner. He'd had only one accident in the house. He hadn't destroyed anything. What more could I ask for? And why *didn't* I love him yet? What was wrong with me?

I was obviously a terrible person, and that's why I was alone to begin with. Only my cat could tolerate me—and he and I both knew that should something happen to me, he would not hesitate to eat my face.

The problem wasn't him. The problem was that, like the Grinch, my heart had grown two sizes too small.

I could barely take care of myself, and I was suddenly responsible for another life form a lot more dependent than my cat. Did I need an animal trailing me from room to room, never more excited than when I got up to go fix a cup of tea?

It wasn't supposed to be this way. In all those chick lit books, where the spunky heroine is dealing with her singleness, she has a quirky canine keeping her company (whom she adores, of course).

The truth is that all those people who tell you to get a dog because you've recently lost a relationship partner seem to think that the dog is suddenly going to fill that hole. After all, you won't be coming home to an empty house.

I am here to tell it to you plainly: *a dog does not replace your relationship*. It won't, all of a sudden, cure you of your broken heart—and that was my problem. My heart was still broken. I was a mess.

That's not to say Simon wasn't cute. That's also not to say that I didn't buy him a toy every time I went out, and finally, he had a toy box upstairs and downstairs. (He'd never had a toy before coming to live with me.) I appreciated his enthusiasm in the morning, the way he'd play while I did the morning dishes, the way he began to learn me—and slowly, we settled into each other.

He was patient. Waiting me out.

"Do you love your dog yet?" my friend would ask.

It always pissed me off. "Don't pressure. Love takes time."

The truth is, it took time to feel *anything* other than the misery in which I'd been swimming. But slowly, through my responsibilities to this animal I'd chosen to take in, parts of my frozen bits began to thaw. Daily walks in 30-degree weather, in the rain, picking up dog poop in little plastic bags, coaxing him into the tub by climbing in half naked with treats in hand, administering medicine, standing in the back yard in a bathrobe and winter coat late at night coaxing him to, "Go pee, dammit. We are NOT going for a walk after midnight in THIS neighborhood." Slowly, you realize you are thinking about something other than your misery. His antics make you laugh. The way he will wiggle on his back and try to nibble his own feet from the sheer ecstasy of having his belly rubbed. Your heart warms when he realizes that he can wriggle his nearly 50-lb bulk partway onto your lap. He has every faith in the world that you will rub his belly forever and ever, and when you stop, he instantly forgives you. Your cat headbutts him in the morning, licking his ears and head, and he wags his tail. That's when it happens. Just like that. You get him out of the tub one day, wrap him in a towel, and calm his shivering by rocking him on your lap. He is looking at you with trust in his eyes, surrendering, and you realize that he is helping you to unlock your heart again.

No matter what, for better or for worse, my life is less empty than it was. I may not be a dog person—or a dog for that matter—but thankfully, I am a SIMON person.

I also tell him about James. "If you ever see this man," I say, "you have my permission to bite him."

He won't of course. He will only want to have his belly rubbed, but a gal can dream, right?

SECOND QUARTER
(MONTHS 4 – 6)

CHAPTER 9

**CURSING TORTILLAS AND NAVIGATING
EVERYDAY REMINDERS OF LOVE**

FACT: THE GROCERY store is a florescent-lit minefield.

I was forever buying James edible gifts, working under the mistaken impression that the way to a man's heart is through his stomach—a stomach filled with cheese, to be exact. His favorite was Blue Stilton, with veins so thick it looked like a wedge of marble. But in a pinch, Yancy's Horseradish Cheddar Wheels would do, or Salemville's Amish blue cheese (from cows that are milked twice daily!), or Triple Crème Bri—perhaps a fine Brillat-Savarin with a thick, velvety white crust. Who wouldn't want to eat a cheese named after the author of *Physiologie du gout* (Physiology of Taste), who wrote, "Tell me what you eat and I will tell you what you are."

So, James was cheese. And Round London Broil Roast Beef, thinly sliced. He was Genoa Salami, thick with white lumps of fat. He was Low Sodium Triscuits and High Fiber Tortillas whose net carbs were less than sixteen.

Then there were the beverages. Peach and Tropical Fruit and Raspberry Fruition. Green Machine. Eight O'clock Columbian Ground coffee. Minute Maid Pomegranate. Vanilla Muscle Milk. The always-present Dr. Pepper, hangover cure extraordinaire—take with two Burger King Rodeo burgers and call me in the morning.

Next, an array of frozen pizzas: Newman's Own Roasted Garlic and Chicken; California Pizza Kitchen Hawaiian; Four Cheese; Di-

Giorno's Tuscan Style Spinach, Mushroom, and Garlic; Bacon Blitz; Fire Roasted Peppers, Tomato, and Spinach.

An assortment of condiments: pesto sauce, Sriracha Hot Chili sauce, spicy and exotic mustards. Add to that, mixed nuts. Popcorn. Almond milk for his Kashi Go Lean Crunch cereal. Udon soup. Tamari. Carrots, spinach, onions, Roma tomatoes, asparagus, roasted Brussels sprouts. Pork to be stirred in to his favorite stir fry, poured over his seemingly bottomless bin of bulk brown rice. Celery with a generous coating of Jif peanut butter.

Chips and salsa. Always white corn, sometimes wedges or scoops or strips or artisan, flavored or unflavored coupled with Green Mountain Gringo Medium Salsa, or Desert Pepper Salsa Del Rio ("perched precariously between relentless heat and refreshing cool")—never to be outdone by the favored Newman's Own Pineapple Salsa.

I was not the world's greatest cook, but I made a baddass quesadilla, with plain yogurt in place of sour cream and fresh pico de gallo I made myself with cubed Roma tomatoes, onions, cilantro, lemon juice, minced garlic, a touch of red and green peppers. Every tap of my knife to the cutting board expressed the rhythm of love.

Finally, there was the beer to wash it all down. An ocean of beer. Samual Adams. Negra Modela. Sierra Nevada. Columbus Pale Ale. Molsen. Great Lakes Commodore Perry sailing the IPA seas in a six pack.

But that was then.

Now, trips to the grocery store exclude entire aisles for which I have no use. My needs are small and simple. There is no point in wandering the aisles looking for things that might bring a smile to his face—even if that smile didn't outlast the process of digesting whatever it was I had brought him.

"Fuck you, tortillas," I say, as I walk past them on my way to the paper towels. "Fuck you and the floured conveyer you rode in on.

"As for you, salsa, and your chunks of pineapple mingling with tomatoes and jalapeños, your onions and your allspice, I wouldn't even dip my middle finger in you. What kind of fruit are you to be mixing it up with these vegetables?" Certainly I didn't need this little 16-ounce reminder of late nights spent hearing him talk on and on about himself while dipping chips into jars oozing with spicy sweetness for which I never had the palate.

If the way to his heart had been through his stomach (also first traveling along the overpass of my bank account), then surely I would have been an unexpendable goddess—bringer of all things salty and creamy-cheesy. But his stomach deceived. It grew up and slightly over the waistband of his pants, expanding like the yeast in his beer. His stomach grew larger and not his heart. If only he could have carried me in his stomach, nestled close like a wedge of triple crème brie. If only he could have savored me like a slice of bacon or salami, veined white with fatty goodness. We would still be together—a heart attack and failed liver waiting to happen, but together.

Instead, I indulge myself. Every un-bought, overpriced low-carb zipper pouch of tortillas turns to flowers, a dog toy, those expensive organic blueberry toaster pastries, or...you know...toilet paper and a twelve-pack of light bulbs.

THERE WAS NO longer anyone I could bribe with cheese and roast beef into doing muscle work.

For instance, the chore of changing light bulbs. It seems like such a simple task. Of course, it *is* a simple task—when that light bulb is in a lamp. But wait until it's the light bulb hanging down from your back porch ceiling, which has chosen to burn out after midnight, right as you are about to go to bed. This is a safety issue if you live in a questionable neighborhood, and so you grab the stepstool (now a necessity in your household single person arsenal) and wrestle with the bulb in your bathrobe and slippers. Hurray! Let there be light. (Yes, those are dead moths in your hair.)

Worse, though, are the boob lights. These are the light globes clearly shaped like boobs. There is a (nipple) bolt that holds the globe fixture in place. You unscrew the bolt, slip off the globe, insert the bulb...all while standing on tiptoes on your stepstool, which doesn't quite reach, so your neck is craned upwards at an awkward angle...and then you have to get the globe lined up just right...and contend with a bolt, which incidentally has to fit in the socket THAT YOU CAN'T SEE BECAUSE THERE IS A GIANT GLOBE IN THE WAY! Who thought of these things?! (Some man thinking about boobs, that's who.)

Finally! Let there be light—after only thirty minutes of wrangling with the bolt. (Yes, that's a pinched nerve causing that pain in your neck.)

If you were not self-sufficient before, and if you don't happen to have a lot of strapping male friends, you must now become very ingenious. There will be a greater sense of pride in your accomplishments, but there will also be a lot of cursing, and possibly injuries to self. Now, there are things I look around at and thank the heavens that James did them *before* the breakup—like hanging all those mini-blinds (required drilling), or installing the new bathroom faucet—which appeared to require a lot of grunting beneath the sink cabinet. Now that you are on your own, here are some things in which you might want to invest:

- *Tools:* This is obvious. Bare minimum, you should already have a hammer, drill, drill bits, screwdrivers, good scissors, measuring tape, and nails on hand. If you want to get crazy, add a few wrenches, wire cutters, various bolts and screws, Allen wrenches, thread seal tape (never know when your shower will start spritzing all over the place), toolbox, wood glue, Gorilla Glue, and a treasure trove of 3M hooks. If you can hang it on a 3M hook, count yourself lucky. I've also discovered the secret of screw hooks. You can use these in varying sizes to hang things like spring tension curtain rods. You don't need to drill! Just pound a large nail to start a hole, remove the nail, and then you can screw the screw hook into the wall.

- *Stepstool:* They make these great ones that are plastic and fold up for storage. I use mine all the time, or I climb up on my kitchen stool, but hey…that's me living dangerously (yes, I have fallen).

- *Light bulbs:* If you live alone and need outdoor lighting for safety, try to have these on hand at all times. You can also now get porch lights with built-in motion sensors, which take regular bulbs. (Also, you can change the orientation of these lights so that access to the bulb is on the BOTTOM rather than the top. This makes all the difference in the world when it's late at night and you can't see because…uh, the porch light isn't working.)

- *Spare keys:* Have you ever locked yourself out of the house when no one has a spare key? I have. (Not once but twice, actually.) I also had to use the bathroom pretty badly at the time, and there was no way to break into my house. My call to the landlord (I had my cell phone at least) went unanswered, and for the briefest of panicked moments, I almost thought about calling James, who still had a key because he'd never bothered to return it. In the end, I had to call a locksmith. I waited thirty minutes for him to arrive. He drove up in an unmarked car, pulled a bag of tools from his trunk, and went to work on my door like a thief. There was nothing to indicate that he wasn't actually a thief. He popped the lock in under three minutes and charged me $100. (Definitely a thief.) It was an expensive lesson. Either leave a key with a friend or find a safe and secure hidey hole for a spare.

- *AAA:* Maybe you had a boyfriend who would have been kind enough to pick you up if your car broke down, you got a flat tire, locked yourself out, ran out of gas, left your lights on and ran your car battery down, or otherwise got into some FUBAR situation with your car. Well...not anymore. Who ya gonna call now? AAA, that's who. Also, they tow. A membership will cost you between $55 and $135 a year—well worth it.

- *Cell phone:* If you don't have one of these—seriously? All right. I'm going to pretend that you didn't admit to it. If you don't have one, you should now get one. How would I have called a locksmith without this? Regardless, you shouldn't leave your house without it. This isn't about updating Facebook while you're driving (please don't do that). This is about being able to call someone in an emergency. (Like a locksmith, AAA, 911, or to check for directions when you get lost because you're always getting lost—or maybe that's just me.)

- *Security system:* If you live alone, it can bring you a lot of peace of mind to install a security system. If you rent, this can be challenging. Companies like ADT charge an arm and a leg, and most likely, you don't have any spares. Thankfully, there are alternatives. Simplisafe offers a system for renters—it's wireless, customizable, you can take it with you, there are no contracts, and you can get 24-hour monitoring for as little as $20 per month. It also comes with a panic button. It's totally worth the upfront investment (about $300 if you have a medium-sized house) for the peace of mind.

- *Stun gun or Pepper spray*: If you don't feel comfortable owning a gun (and I normally recommend the rule that if you don't feel comfortable with the idea of firing one or killing someone, then you shouldn't have one that can be used against you), a stun gun or pepper spray can be good alternatives. You can get a small stun gun for carrying with you and a large one for home defense. Stun batons can be especially good because they have an extended reach, you don't have to be in close proximity, and it's hard for them to grab it away from you. The Guard Dog Taser is one of my personal favorites for outside of the home. It works as an incredibly bright flashlight, has a ridged edge that will break glass, and also works as a 4.5 million stun gun. You can carry this openly without people realizing you are armed. Some people prefer Pepper Spray because it has a long range and can have a devastating effect. Typically, if someone gets it in their eyes, it can be very debilitating. Just make sure you are upwind!

- *Google:* I am dead serious. This is a tool. I mean, what did I do before Google? I called people on the phone who never knew the answer, that's what. Seriously, if you don't know anything about whatever it is you want to know about, chances are you can Google it. This comes in handy if you own your house instead of rent. If you rent, call the landlord. Hopefully, you have a decent one who will actually repair things. If you own, then Google is your friend. So is your local hardware store.

- *Hardware store:* Believe it or not, you can sometimes get good service at these places, including instructions on how to do certain things (that you read about on Google). Now is the time to expand your knowledge. It's an excellent time filler, and there really is some satisfaction to be had in completing tasks yourself. The clerks at my local Lowe's practically know me by name.

Look, I don't need you, is what I think whenever I'm able to accomplish something on my own. Funny how I also think, *Dammit, what a jerk you are,* whenever there's something I *can't* do on my own. But it passes. The great thing about this new state of being is that it can force you out of your shell. There are going to be some occasions when you will *have* to ask for help. (Like that time I hit the light pole behind my house with my car, knocking the metal pole out of alignment and exposing the wiring. No way could I move the pole back in place on my own. Thankfully, Roy's son was willing to lend a hand. Not-so-thankfully, he waited around after in a way that suggested he might want a date rather than just a heartfelt thank you.)

Roy still mows my lawn and has yet to accept money from me. He seems satisfied with cookies and the hand-me-downs consisting of things I'm slowly getting rid of in my house. Brad (my other neighbor) once spent twenty minutes helping me break into my house (in the rain, no less) after I locked myself out (for the second time). In a world that seems callous and cruel, there are moments when we can discover the exact opposite. There is kindness in the world if we open ourselves to it. There are people willing to be in service to others, and our own vulnerability has a way of making us more willing to be in service in return—that is, unless we're too busy hiding out in our house still wearing pajamas and watching *High Fidelity* over and over again.

If you *are* hiding out in your pajamas watching breakup flicks while sobbing into a pizza box, then this means you've settled into Boo-hooville. Let's see what we can do about getting you out.

THERE WAS CERTAINLY a reason I packed my bags and left (figuratively speaking, since he was the one to do the actual bag-packing and subsequent leaving). I wanted out of Crazytown. This was that place where I found myself driving around in my car, aimlessly, at four o'clock in the morning wondering where James was. The gig was over. The bars were closed. Why hadn't he returned my call or responded to my text message *this* time? Some nights, I would find myself in a grocery store parking lot, just sitting in my car, desperately needing to be anywhere but home, thinking, *This craziness is not me.*

And so,

one

graceless

dismount

later, here I was. Certainly *not* in Crazytown. Only, this new place, this Boo-hooville, was a dump!

First of all, there didn't seem to be many people out wandering around wearing smiles. The other inhabitants of this not-so-fine city were, like I, too mired in their own misery to come out of their little caves and so much as wave hello at a neighbor. "Can I get a cup of sugar?"

Hell no. All we've got here are a whole lot of pillars of salt.

Another drawback: No one wants to come visit you here. Pretty much people only want to know when you plan to leave.

"Are you done yet?" they ask.

"Done what?"

"Done grieving over that creep. You know, the guy who neglected you and made you crazy all the time. That one."

"Oh," you say.

"Oh?"

"Well…uh…not exactly."

And this is the truth, because this particular location is hard to escape. No amount of "Screw that guy, and can I key his car?" from well-meaning friends and relatives can motivate you to head for the state line.

You can't move on because this place requires that you get some work done first.

Closure.

Oh, not with him. That may never happen. You have to get this with yourself.

What I really want (if I can't have him crawling back to me telling me how much he really does love me and how he's sorry that he treated me so poorly and how he's going to work on himself and grow) is for him to realize that I was awesome to him (for the most part) and bought him great food (see Cursing Tortillas) and was pretty amazing overall (except when I was trying desperately to get his love and grew a little crazy from my failure to do so), and that he is…

Wait. That he DOES love me, how he's sorry that he treated me so poorly and how he's going to work on himself and grow.

That's probably not closure. Neither is simply getting angry and screaming, "I'm better off and screw that guy" from the rooftops—no matter how much you think it might make everything better.

It isn't fair. Let me say this again. It isn't fair. It just isn't. No amount of anything is going to make it fair. Boo-hoo. (Boo-hoo, by the way, is the slogan you'll find posted on the Welcome sign when you tumble into town. "Welcome to Boo-hooville. Population Who Gives a Damn.")

It's not fair. I LOVED that guy. I loved him with all my heart. What more can be said than that? Nothing. It's so inadequate. Just to say, "I loved that guy, and it didn't work out," is like the understatement of the century to the brokenhearted. The feelings behind the words are so crushing that the words themselves are infuriating in their inadequacy to convey anything meaningful. You want to make it about more than this, but it's really not. You loved that guy, and it didn't work out.

Worse, that crushing pain makes it difficult to remember your reasons for wanting to leave Crazytown in the first place. When you compare Crazytown to Boo-hooville, well, Crazytown appears to win, hands-down. After all, there was at least *some* good to be had there, at least occasionally. Here? Not so much. What was a little day-to-day sadness compared to *this* enormous creature chomping away on your body, mind, and soul day and night?

The answer is that you did not leave Crazytown for Boo-hooville. Boo-hooville is a layover. It is a temporary stop. It is the dismal Greyhound bus station in the first leg of your trip to Kauai. It is a place you must visit on your way to peace and calm. It is a rough stone that you will use to scrape away the old skin so that you can be made new again. And yes, that scraping hurts. And yes, you look terrible while it's happening. Everything is dropping off, wrinkling, sagging, and flaking; it's dull-colored. But underneath? On the other side of that? It's beautiful.

For me, Boo-hooville is also a place of hard truths—but they are at least Obvious Truths. In this new place, I don't have to wonder what time he's coming home. (Never.) Or feel anxiety because he's not responding to my text message where I said I loved him. (Because he doesn't love me back.) No one is yelling at me, or telling me to "Shut the fuck up." No one is telling me what I ought to be doing. *I am doing* what I ought to be doing, which is whatever it is I happen to be doing. If I want to put on pajamas at two in the afternoon, then so be it. (I don't, by the way, but I'm just saying I *could*.)

There is only one way out of Boo-hooville, and that's through it. No shortcuts. No bypass. No outerbelt. Straight through.

CHAPTER 12
OVERCOMING EMOTIONAL DISPARITY:
A WEREWOLF ON MY FRIDGE

CERTAINLY, IT MIGHT have been much easier to exit Boo-hooville if I'd had someone delicious and yummy encouraging me to leave. But there wasn't anyone. What's more, I couldn't even *picture* it. Every time I tried to imagine someone other than James in my house, in my bed, laughing with me and holding my hand, I drew a blank.

For someone who believes in the power of visualization, this was a source of never-ending frustration. How could I possibly begin to attract someone new if I couldn't even *imagine* someone new? Then something very simple occurred to me. I was nowhere near ready to attract someone new. That's why I couldn't picture it.

Terribly lonely as I was, I was currently better off on my own.

Really?

Ugh.

That's right. The words you don't want to hear when you're lonely and sad and your self-esteem has drifted to somewhere well below sea level—like maybe down to where those aliens in the movie *Abyss* reside—and you feel that the only way to reclaim your heart and your dignity will be if someone else actually tells you how incredibly filled with awesomesauce you are, preferably while they are getting you naked.

But it doesn't work like that. Not really.

This may not be a case of "If you fall off the horse, jump right back on." Honestly, it might *not* be a good idea to jump right back on. Chances are pretty good that you fell off the horse because

1. You're not a very good rider.

2. The horse didn't want you on its back.

3. Shit happens; i.e., there was a low-hanging tree branch, the horse stumbled, maybe the horse was headed for a cliff and you didn't feel like going over the edge with it.

The chances are *also* good that you have some minor (or major) injuries as a result of this fall. If you're just a little banged up, then you probably don't need this book. You'll eat some Ben and Jerry's tonight and be back to all systems go by morning. But if your breakup had a monumental impact on your life, it's because you were on a wild romp courtesy of your raging heartstallion, and now you are experiencing the aftereffects of getting bucked.

So I'd fallen (probably for all three of the reasons listed above), and I couldn't visualize getting back up onto *anything*. There is a saying: "The best way to get over someone is to get under someone new." Well, I'm not here to be the moral police, and the truth is that some people do very well with this approach. At least, they *think* they do. As noted before, this is because it takes the edge off of the chemical withdrawal. But at some point, especially if there were true and deep emotions involved, or someone got very hurt in the process, then there will come a time when you must pay your dues. You will have to account for it one way or another—even if it's not to the person you hurt or who hurt you; even if you think you are moving on, chances are good that you are simply carting an additional set of baggage into your next relationship. What happened in your last relationship is bound to creep into your current one unless you pause to resolve the issues that might have played a role in the dissolution to begin with. Believe me when I tell you this: both parties are culpable.

This means taking inventory. What is in there anyway? ("In there" being in *you*.) What happened? If you hurt someone pretty badly, then you need to take inventory. Can you own any part of having hurt them? If you are hurting pretty badly, then you need to take inventory. Can you own any part of allowing yourself to be hurt so badly? How easily can you move forward now? If it's difficult, it suggests that you are still tied to this person in some way. These may be psychic ties. They must be released one way or another. If you have hurt someone, you may need to atone before you can move forward with someone new. (This doesn't necessarily mean that you have to contact that person directly, because in some cases this may not be appropriate; however, you may find yourself in a place where you need to ask their forgiveness and also forgive yourself.) If, on the other hand, someone has hurt you deeply, you may have to forgive *that person* before you can move forward with someone new.

I was most certainly still taking inventory. I couldn't even get to the point where I could feel attracted to others. I needed to let go and reclaim myself. More than my heart had broken; it felt like my body had died. In addition to all the other indignities I was suffering at the hands of this breakup, I was also now forced to consider the fact that my body simply hadn't gotten the memo. "Yo! You're not *his* anymore," I wanted to tell it. "You can look at other men." Only, it just didn't seem that simple. I didn't want other men. I still wanted him.

Sort of.

Not.

But yes, I did.

Only if he were nicer. And maybe, uh…loved me back.

Enter Alcide.

In the early stages of the breakup, I spent a lot of time watching the HBO series *True Blood*. Every season there was, in fact (which at the time was only two). It was the only show that could distract me from my crushing sadness. And while everyone was going crazy over vampires and fairies and shapeshifters, I was more interested in a certain werewolf. He was strong, protective, manly, all those things I was looking for in the moment. He was a guardian angel of sorts (with a five o'clock shadow). Here was the quality I desperately craved in my sadness—a highly protective alpha male.

While naturally I could not have *him*—fictional TV character that he was—I needed the energy of what he represented. So, I printed out a picture of him and tacked it to my fridge. It was a reminder: Yes, you will find other men attractive. Yes, there are actually other men—not just a city full of red minivans, which may or may not contain the man who was never yours to begin with. Indeed, there are even other men who have many positive qualities—not the least of which may be their capacity to adore you as much as you adore them. Look, maybe someday, you'll get a man who is a little like the one currently tacked to your fridge—although probably minus the werewolf bit.

A girl can dream, can't she? I mean, that's the point: visualization!

Alcide eventually gave way to all things Mark Ruffalo (look, I'm not laughing at who *you* have tacked to *your* refrigerator…), and before I knew it, my fridge had turned into a collage of sorts depicting my changing life. I bought a lot of magnets, and whenever I saw an image (or took a picture) that resonated with me, that moved something in me, I tacked it to the fridge where I was bound to see it frequently. It served not only as a reminder of what it was that I wanted or was drawn to, but it is also served as a visual record of the ways in which my life was no longer what it had been with James.

So, on those days when I feel as if nothing is happening, I can look at this and be reminded that things *have* changed, at least a little, and that I am also actively moving toward something—even if it's only in my imagination. (Trust me: this is where all things actually begin.)

But of course, there is the flip-side of despairing over the inability to picture another man in your life. You are also not quite so sure it's worth trying to love again in the first place. I call this little mind monster *the Jabberwocky of emotional disparity.*

Suddenly, I found myself right on the brink of becoming bitter about love—love, which now seemed to hold up as well as a sheet of rice paper in a hurricane. Love, which appeared to have the life span of a fruit fly.

There is something critical to learn about love: It's not like it's portrayed in all those romantic comedies or Nicholas Sparks' books. It's easy to get so caught up in visions of romantic love that when its real life counterpart comes along, it's difficult not to become disappointed. And yet, when love is over—even painful love—it still feels like *life* is over.

My heart doesn't really like being dead. I imagine this to be a somewhat universal sentiment. I mean, assuming we're not sociopaths, human beings tend to gravitate toward love. But in order to heal, we eventually have to reach the point where we stop thinking that it is the end of the world that our ex-partner does not love us. The fact of the matter is, if indeed that love no longer exists—or never existed to begin with—then it's *to our benefit* to move on. A relationship takes work, and if both people aren't willing to engage in that work, it's unlikely that what we are building in our lives will be useful to anyone but the one doing the building. The good news is that it *is* still actually useful. We can keep building—we might simply need to rethink the plans.

> "The lover who abides belongs to the future, to the eternal. From the angle of the future, the break is not really a break, but rather a possibility. But the powers of the eternal are needed for this. The lover must abide in love, otherwise the heartache of the past still has the power to keep alive the break" (Kierkegaard, *Provocations*).

At this point, it's also useful to spend time thinking about healthy needs vs. *un*healthy needs. For instance, if you need for someone to tell you they love you every ten minutes in order to believe it (because they might change their mind at any moment), then this might be an unhealthy need. I wouldn't recommend voicing this need to anyone but your therapist. The function of a relationship partner is not to follow us around on our own personal schedule and validate us. They can encourage us, yes. But if we rely on them as our sole source of validation, or as the only source of good feelings, then we are dooming our relationship to failure—and then, in times when we're without them (like now), we are *desperate* for validation from just about *anyone*.

Look at yourself in the mirror. I mean really *look*. I bet that there is something about you that you find beautiful. Go deeper than that. Consider the fact that everyone on this planet, even Buddhist masters and priests and medicine men and Joan of Arc experienced spiritual doubt and suffering. They had to learn how best to relate to others. They had to work on themselves in order to accomplish anything of greatness. If any of them are reasonable, they will all tell you that the project of the self is one that never ends. It is never safe to let down your guard and say, "Ah! Yes! I'm done. I couldn't better a single other thing about myself." (If you encounter such a person, punch him in the face. Not really, but certainly it's okay to picture it.)

Do you think that some people are more worthy of love than others? Do you think you are *less* worthy of love because your body doesn't resemble that of a Photoshopped underwear model and you are also definitely weird? Do you think you are *less* worthy of love because you are needy, or prone to feeling lonely and wonder whether you will wind up the old cat lady in a rocking chair knitting afghan caps for concrete lawn ducks? You probably *are* a little bit crazy. How can you be a thinking person and not also be a little bit crazy? You're probably also a little bit neurotic, and most definitely narcissistic. I bet you have some strange beliefs about things. I bet you can be arrogant. I bet you can be a bit mean when you want to be, and inconsiderate, too. I am all of these things as well. The best thing we can do is realize it. Own it. Do what we can to become better. If you are doing that, to the best of your ability, then you are worthy of love. If someone doesn't want to be with you because they think you're too difficult to deal with, then I'm guessing there is another person out there who will probably think the opposite. (And even *their* opinion doesn't really matter.)

Do you know how many people are on this planet? Approximately 7 billion. Those are really excellent odds. The days of being limited in choice by geographic proximity are long gone. There are other fish in the sea, and the sea is much bigger. (Especially now that there are sites like Facebook, and Match.com, and Chemistry.com, and eHarmony, and…you get the idea…)

When you feel the most crazy—the most lonely, or uncertain, or fearful regarding the future—try to redirect the energy. Sometimes, when we're feeling something overwhelming, we can literally feel it in our bodies. We hold our emotions in any number of places—our backs, shoulders, stomachs, foreheads… Try doing something creative, or try exercising. Unfortunately, this probably means some form of vigorous exercise, which will cause you to breathe heavily. I'll tell you a secret though—when you're just trying to take a deep breath, you're not wondering whether anyone might ever see you naked again.

It's probably long overdue for us to throw out what we think we know about love. Girls have grown up with too many fairy tale/date movies/romance bodice-rippers racing around in our heads—the warrior with his rippling muscles and the golden-maned damsel clinging to his breeches. The title is something like *Savage Heat* or *Destiny's Desire*. This is the fairy tale world where men and women always orgasm at the same time or where the man wakes the sleeping princess with a kiss, or where the hero slays the dragon and rescues the damsel from a tower, or where, essentially, everyone lives happily ever after and no one writes what happens next.

What happens next is that *reality* sets in. The golden bubble bursts. There are bills to pay. Someone has to walk the dog and clean the cat litter box and go to the grocery store for milk. Real love involves real life, with real moods, individual needs and problems, and baggage we're all trying to manage.

The Prince Charmings of the world are the ones who love you for who you truly are. That's it. I'll take that over dragon-slaying any day.

Times have changed. After all, I'm daydreaming about werewolves, and it's beginning to look as if I'll have to climb the tower myself in order to rescue…uh…my*Self*.

From what?

From zombies.

YES. IT IS. Some of the thoughts running around in your brain are little zombie brain-munchers. If you look at the wrinkles in your forehead, you won't be able to see them, but trust me: it's the walking dead in there.

There will come a time when all you can think about is how wrong this whole thing is. It shouldn't be this way. What more could you have done to get/gain/keep his love? If there is another woman involved, you will wonder what she has that you do not have. And how could he have chosen her over you? And how could he have moved on so quickly, with no looking back? If there was abuse, you may wonder how he could have done those things to you. Worst of all, you may have to face some of these supposed truths:

I loved him. He did not love me.
I had hoped we would get/stay married and be happy together.
It is over and we will never speak again.
I am alone. I'll always be alone. I deserve to be alone.
This isn't fair!

But the truth is a little bit tricky when it comes to the ego. The ego assigns the value of truth to things that are, in actuality, stories—usually horror stories, but stories nonetheless. Truth (with a capital T) isn't necessarily all that difficult to spot when we put our minds to it (and turn on our bullshit detectors). Usually, we can examine our thoughts against reality and spot the falsehoods right off. This, by the way, is the first step in locating those brain-munching zombies.

I loved him. / *True. Always will on some level.*

We are not together right now. / *True. 'Cause I am in my house, and there's only the dog and cat here with me. Probably also some spiders and a few gnats I saw buzzing around.*

I am alone; I'll always be alone. / *Ah! This is false. I mean, there are the dog and cat and the spiders and gnats I mentioned. I am romantically alone, is what the ego meant.*

I deserve to be alone. / *Absolutely! Isn't it great? I mean, seriously, what a relief to finally have some time to myself where I'm not all filled with anxiety or crying because he said something mean or waking up in the middle of the night because he's coming in drunk again and banging things around or…wait a minute. That's right. I was busy feeling* bad *about being alone.*

What is happening here is that we are wallowing in mind mud. This is our pained ego trying to drag itself up from the dark well in which we find ourselves, although really it's only succeeding in pulling us further down.

How do you battle the ego? I did a Google search, and I had a hard time finding precise instructions! Also, my ego barely had the patience to read any of it. It didn't really have a motive to find the answer. It likes to sabotage. It likes to stay in charge, even though most of the time, it really makes a terrible mess of things. When it feels hurt in any way, it acts like a three-year-old and throws a tantrum of the worst sort, and if I'm not careful, it will carry me along for the ride. Right to the bottom of a river, really. It doesn't mind killing me off in its desperation to be the one in charge. Martyrdom at its finest!

Thankfully, I've sneaked a few books past my ego and learned the following: To battle the ego, the first thing you have to do is recognize when the voice you are hearing is Ego. When the wounding is to your Ego more so than your soul, the part of you that is incredibly resilient and beautiful and beyond the reach of mere mortals who may break your heart and hurt you along the path of life, then the pain you feel is perpetuated quite horrifically by a lot of extraneous building upon reality with dark-tinged fantasy.

Let's examine those previous statements again, shall we?

I loved him. **He did not love me.**

Oh boo! Can I really know this? Am I inside his head? This is the zombie-munched portion of brain talking. It is turning me into a pouty-brat.

I have been hurt badly, yes; but most likely, I have been hurt badly by his *negligence*.

Let me expound here upon the concept of negligence. My brilliant lawyer friend, Barbara, has this to say on the subject:

"...try to keep in mind how messy life is, how messed up we can all act from time to time, and how easy it is to run roughshod over someone else's feelings or life without hardly noticing. The someone-run-roughshod-over may, of course, be hurt and feel betrayed and long for an apology or explanation or SOME-THING, but, you know, we didn't notice the offense or didn't realize what we did was an offense and anyway, life is messy, and we didn't mean to hurt anyone...ever. This unconcerned getting on with life, or not noticing, or failure to otherwise take some remedial action can make the someone-run-roughshod-over believe that our actions and inactions are *not* a result of us being merely negligent or careless but are evidence of our *malice*. We enjoyed inflicting the pain and enjoy the many, many ramifications now and forever and ever. Muah-hah-hah-hahhh....

"More often than not, the person or entity was acting (or failing to act) out of sheer everyday garden variety cluelessness (or, in the case of an entity, bureaucratic clusterfuckery). Oddly enough, it turns out that people would *rather* believe the malice bit than believe that they were simply...not considered at all. Perhaps that's why our minds turn so eagerly to attributing malice to those things done to us unintentionally, which hurt us so badly. It's too annoyingly painful to believe that we can be so hurt and so brought down by someone who hurt us or brought us down *unthinkingly*. As if our pain was not obvious to them. As if we are not their focus. As if we were not the primary (or secondary or tertiary) reason they did what they did (or failed to do what they failed to do)."

Urff. She is right. Pure negligence. Unlike malice, it means he is busy living his own life, not making choices based on what he thinks will hurt me the most. Even if he *were* acting out of malice, well…so what? It changes my reality hardly at all—**only the story I tell myself about that reality**.

I had hoped we would get married.
It is over **and we will never speak again.**

This is another thing I can't possibly know. It's over all right. Yes. True. The rest sounds sad, doesn't it? Dramatic. *Housewives of Orange County* and the long pause before all those reality TV shows give you the results on who's going home dramatic.

It is over, America, and………………...…we will…………………
never speak…………………….again.

Blargh! We're not speaking right this second. I know that much. Beyond that, I cannot know.

I am alone. **I'll always be alone. I deserve to be alone.**

I'm sad for her! Ego wants someone yummy telling her how lovely and loved she is. She is really hoping someone might refute this statement. If not, she will belly up to the fires of anger and bitterness to warm herself. If we can't punish the people we deem responsible for our terrible feelings, then we'll punish ourselves with a lot of poisonous thinking. Bleck!

This isn't fair.

Of course it is! It is perfectly fair! Do you want to know why? Because I had a very large hand in helping to create this moment. You might even say that every moment of my life lived thus far has been leading up to this moment. This rather perfect moment, I might add. I *know* it's a struggle to believe that this moment is perfect. Especially *this* moment:

> You are lying on the kitchen floor, mud on your pants, sobbing your eyes out—even though it's been six months already. The tears are not just for him but also for the fact that it's been six months, and you can't believe you're crying on the kitchen floor when you should, possibly, be naked in bed with the man of your dreams. Or at the least, eating copious amounts of ice cream. But nope. Reality check. You are still lactose intolerant. Also, you are most certainly on the floor, muddy, crying your eyes out because your heart hurts. Because your skin is so radiantly sensitive to life right now that even the lightest touch of wind is almost painful.

THIS is the moment I'm talking about. Don't try to make it something else. Don't fight it. You don't have to tell yourself to "buck up, little bunny." You don't have to tell yourself that he's an asshole and he didn't deserve you. Maybe he did and maybe he didn't, but the truth is also that you LOVED that asshole, and—admit it—you gave what you gave willingly. So now it's over, and it hurts, and you're crying on the floor, and that is *perfectly okay.*

I'm serious. It's *perfectly okay to hurt like this. You are so beautiful hurting like this. I am deeply connected to you right now hurting like this.*

I promise you that in a little while, you'll stop crying. You'll get up, wipe your nose with the nearest thing handy (maybe the sleeve of your shirt), get something to drink, and go on with your day. It may not all be sunshine and roses, and you may not have a lot to smile about, but that's okay, too. It's the ego doing all this grasping and could've, would've, should've kind of talk.

Next, now that you've identified Ego when you hear its voice, let's talk about how to remove the zombie bits from your otherwise perfectly lovely brain.

The majority of advice out there has to do with being contrary to the negative thoughts running through our heads. (So, being negative to the negativity? Negating the negativity? Hmm…) For example, the moment you think something like, "I bet his family prefers her to me because she can eat Burger King," you must fire back with something like, "I am lovely and smart and deserve love."

Bullocks! That doesn't work for me. Want to know why? Because when I'm busy thinking something horrible about myself, it's pretty tough to come up with something good *that I will believe* in that moment. It's true! I can't eat Burger King. What's more, I don't *want* to eat Burger King. Gee, that Burger King is doing unflattering things to everyone's waistline. So why would I want to become a slovenly, grease-coated slob? (Still Ego talking, by the way. Firing back nastiness. Take that! Bang-bang! Munch-munch!)

Alternatively, consider the following statement:

Thank you for everything; I have no complaint whatsoever.

This comes from a Zen parable about a man who goes up a hill to see a Zen Master about a problem. (I have refreshed the parable a bit for the modern age…)

One day, a terribly sad and lonely man traveled to a distant land (Carmel Valley, CA) to see a Zen Master for some much-needed advice. He used the last of his money to take a plane, a taxi, and then a Stage for the final 14 miles of mountain dirt road with its sheer drop-offs and vertical cliffs. Finally, he arrived at the Master's cabin (where there was no cell reception or wifi) and told him this story:

"Master, my life is pretty awful. My wife left me for another man. In the divorce, she also got the house and most of my money. The whole thing gave me an ulcer, and I missed so many days of work that I lost my job. I can only afford a cheap apartment in a terrible neighborhood. I can hear gunfire some nights, and when I'm not hearing gunfire, I'm hearing the trains passing right near my house, and the walls shake so much that I can't sleep. I don't know what to do." The man dropped his head in his hands, too sad even to cry.

The Master listened patiently as the man spoke, then smiled at him and said, "Each morning when you wake up, each afternoon when you eat your lunch, and each night before you go to bed, pause and say, 'Thank you for everything; I have no complaint whatsoever.'"

The man felt quite dubious about this prescription. (He was already beginning to regret having spent his meager savings to travel someplace where he couldn't update his Facebook status, Tweet about all the people walking around barefoot, check game scores, or use Google Voice to locate the nearest McDonald's), but the energy of the man in front of him was so peaceful and filled with joy that he agreed to try it.

Three months later, the man found himself making the journey once more.

"Master," he said, "I did as you asked. Each morning, afternoon, and night, I said precisely what you told me to say, and yet my wife refuses to come back to me, I'm still out of work, living with my brother-in-law, and their fold-out couch is doing very bad things to my back. In short, my life still kind of sucks. What else have you got?"

The Master only smiled and said, "Thank you for everything; I have no complaint whatsoever."

The man returned home enlightened.

"What do you mean?" you might be saying. "His life still sounded awful!"

Well, the point of all this is that your ego's version of perfection and the reality of life don't always jive. Let's face it: they *rarely* jive, and this fact may be important. It keeps us striving. It keeps us working on our lives and ourselves. It keeps us creating! But when our ego begins to stop us from growing, when it begins to hold us back, when we begin to feel as if we're *entitled* to something more than what we have without also having to invest *everything* into our own lives and growth as human beings—then we need to stop and take inventory. What is life *truly* like—once we strip away all of the story telling and anger and pain? Can we bring ourselves to say, "Thank you for everything; I have no complaint whatsoever"? This doesn't mean that we should be grateful only because things could be worse (although they could). Nor does it mean that things couldn't be better. It means, *No matter what happens, the answer is, YES.*

I'm on the floor crying? *Yep. That's true.* He's not here anymore? *Absolutely.* He's with someone else, and they are snuggled up together in more Facebook pics? *Hey! I'm here breathing, and that's awesome.*

My ego scoffs. My ego doesn't believe this for a second, but it doesn't have to. I'm keeping it from telling me stories that are 100% fiction (but still feel every bit as real as a kick in the gut by a size-ten boot). I'm encouraging it, with the utmost of kindness, to consider another perspective. Not another story that I'm telling myself about how I'm really beautiful and wonderful and the bees' knees and any man should be honored to have me, yada yada. (Especially when I know that I'm all these things but also some other things that aren't as rosy-smelling.) Or about how he shouldn't have done such-and-such terrible thing to me. How I'm so *justified* in my *righteous* anger. I'm encouraging my ego simply to consider the notion that the way things are RIGHT NOW is actually precisely how they should be.

I have no idea what's around the next bend, and neither does my ego. If I can learn to love what is in the moment, I will be free. But since that's probably still a bit of a ways off, how about this: If I can learn to BE in this moment, then I'm at least not actively hurting myself with stories about things that *aren't actually still happening.* You are reading this book right now, for instance, not being chased by man-eating meerkats. So, it's okay to breathe a little.

Thank you.

CHAPTER 14
BUT HAVE YOU CONSIDERED WHETHER THE UNIVERSE MIGHT ACTUALLY BE TRYING TO KILL YOU?

YES. I HAVE considered this! Wonderful of you to ask.

I'm pretty sure the answer is no. (I mean, it's not like *plotting* or anything...at least, I mean, uh, probably it's not.)

The fact of the matter is that the end of this play has already been written. We know that we are here for a finite amount of time, barring the transformation of ourselves into cyborgs or moving our brains into robotic bodies. We will pass on. But in the meantime, does this mean that the universe doesn't have our best interests in mind?

Depends on what you think of when you think *best interest*. Normally, our view of our own best interest is incredibly narrow and short-sighted. We can't see beyond our own desires, and those desires color everything in varying shades of either rose or black and white. What we think is best for us (i.e., that new pair of shoes we don't need, a convertible we can't afford, an entire large pizza, working ourselves to death, refusing to make changes in our lives when we know they are long overdue, or being carried along on a cushion of ennui without any real purpose) may not be what is best for our SPIRIT. Our spirit can handle quite a bit of what is thrown its way, and generally, rising to the challenges presented by our lives (the universe) can benefit us emotionally and mentally as well as spiritually. But the key here is allowing our spirits to rise to challenges. Often, because this involves things that are UNCOMFORTABLE—at least initially—we rebel. We'd rather sit in the corner and pout than do any real, useful work. I should know. I'm pretty good at pouting.

At some point in your life, you will probably draw a conclusion about the universe (or God). You will decide that it is either benevolent—generally a force for good—or you will decide that it's malevolent—a chaotic force applied simply to spin the accumulated potential energy out of us. There is the middle ground, too: you may also decide that it's a generally disinterested party. It doesn't give two shits for what happens to you, meaning you are pretty much on your own, floundering around in the waves. When you decide this, life becomes a fairly scary place. All kinds of fears rise to the surface because, let's face it, once you figure no one has your back, you spend all your time looking behind you, waiting for someone to creep up and kick you. That is, when you're not busy kicking other people so they can't hurt you first.

I have lost my faith on many occasions. What happens is that my mind begins phrasing thoughts in the following manner:

- *Gee… The universe sure lets a lot of bad things happen (to me).*
- *Didn't I deserve something good after that crap I'd experienced before this?*
- *I thought I'd done everything right, so why isn't anything good coming along?*
- *Why would the universe let this fill-in-the-blank unfortunate thing happen, since it's so obviously shitty?*

Notice the use of "good," "bad," and "unfortunate/shitty" in those thoughts. Also, notice that I'm only thinking about myself. For example, what if this "bad" thing that happened to me was also the "best" thing that could have happened for James? What if this "bad" thing enables me to help others in their lives, right when they need it most? What if this "unfortunate" and "shitty" thing turns out to be a critical growth experience? The short view of my life makes it seem as if, each time something "bad" happens, I am being punished. I am not being rewarded for all the nice things I've done, or the nice things I'm *trying* to do, at least.

Why-oh-why would a benevolent universe want people as awesome as we are to go through all this?

I dunno.

Regardless, we've got some work to do, Scooby Doo.

CHAPTER 15

MAKING MUSIC WITH THE UNIVERSE

IMAGINE THAT EVERYTHING in the universe vibrates—that all of the particles that make up matter and forces are made up of tiny, vibrating strings.[13] This is the concept behind String Theory. Moreover, every one of these strings is identical. The only difference between one string and another, whether it's a heavy particle that is part of an atom or a massless particle that carries light, is its resonant pattern, or how it vibrates.[14]

All objects have resonant patterns. We can understand this best by imagining stringed musical instruments and how their resonant patterns relate to sound.

If you pluck the string of a guitar, you will hear a tone (a steady, periodic sound). Sound is made up of changes in air pressure in the form of waves. That tone you hear is the string's fundamental resonant pattern, or frequency. Frequency is the number of times an event occurs within a specific time period—in this case, it is the frequency of *vibration*. This frequency of vibration is one of the things that help us to determine pitch. When considering the matter of high and low pitches, we are determining how quickly the sound wave is making the air vibrate. This means that a high pitch is a very rapid oscillation and a low pitch is a slower oscillation. Pluck a low E string on a guitar and you can actually see the vibration of the string. If you pluck the high E string on a guitar, it moves so fast you can barely see the vibration.

Yet, it is not just the literal musical string that vibrates! The body of a guitar, for instance, has its own resonant frequencies, which serve to *amplify* the sound created by the vibrating string. This principle applies to non-musical objects as well, albeit in less immediately obvious ways. This book you are holding, for instance, resonates. So does the coffee mug on the table, the TV stand in the living room, the chair in which you are sitting, even the planet—all vibrating.

String Theory also states that the vibrational pattern itself determines what type of particle the string is. One resonant pattern makes it a photon, for example, while another makes it a heavy particle found within the nucleus of an atom.[15]

Einstein, in his famous equation $E=MC^2$, suggested that the more energy something contains, the more mass it has. In String Theory, that means that a lower-energy string is lighter (less mass) and a higher energy string is heavier (more mass). This also points to the fact that it is the frequency of the vibration that determines its energy state rather than its size. Just like our plucked guitar string, the higher the frequency, the more energy (higher pitch/faster oscillation). The lower the frequency, the less energy (lower pitch/slower oscillation).

I know you might be saying something like, "Great! Particle Physics. So...uh...what exactly does this have to do with my breakup?"

Well, it's elementary! (Not really, but bear with me.)

Everything around us is vibrating, producing high and low frequencies, reaching out in every direction in the form of high pressure and low pressure waves. That includes us—we're vibrating, too. Imagine that our thoughts, our intentions, our energy, also travel in similar waves. These things all make up the *frequency* of our vibration. There are the pressure waves that we produce, based on our frequencies, and then there are the pressure waves that are being produced by everything else and their frequencies...let's call these other waves *Universal* waves.

Now, if we imagine that our thoughts and intentions have a direct correlation to our own rate of vibration, then we can also imagine that our very beings are, in a sense, creating music. We aren't the only ones, of course. The universe and everything in it is also creating music. The question is, are we generating low frequencies or high frequencies? Are we creating beautiful harmony or dissonance?

Since we know that the body of a guitar is made to amplify the sounds being created when we pluck the strings, how can we make it so that our bodies, and the body of our thoughts, serve to amplify the higher frequencies of the universe? How can we make certain we're *reinforcing* the higher energy of the universe rather than working contrary to it?

Let's consider a sound wave, or pressure wave, as it relates to *interference*.

We know that sound is made up of changes in air pressure in the form of waves—the result of the back and forth vibration of particles of a medium (such as air) through which the sound wave is traveling. The movement of the wave creates regions in the medium where particles are compressed together and other regions where they are spread apart. This is known as compression and rarefaction. Compressions are regions of high pressure (pulling particles together into small regions) and rarefactions are regions of low pressure (pushing particles apart). **That means a sound wave consists of a repeating pattern of high pressure and low pressure regions moving through a medium.**

So, what happens when two waves encounter each other while traveling along the same medium?

If two high pressure waves meet at the same location, they will *reinforce* each other, creating a region of even *higher* pressure.

If two low pressure waves meet at the same location, they will also *reinforce* each other, creating a region of even *lower* pressure.

But if a high pressure wave and a low pressure wave meet at the same location, they will *cancel each other out*. It will be as if it never occurred. Rather than hearing a louder or softer sound, you would hear no sound at all.

Let's consider this for a moment.

We are vibrating. The universe and everything in it is vibrating. The faster the vibration, the higher the pitch, the more energy is created, and the more instances of high pressure waves or compression (pulling things together). The lower the vibration, the lower the pitch, the less energy is created, and the more instances of low pressure waves or rarefaction (pushing things apart).

If you are vibrating at a low rate, creating low pressures waves, and you encounter other low-vibrating beings and environments, you will actually amplify this energy. That means ***you will create even greater lows.***

If you are vibrating at a high rate, creating high pressure waves, and you encounter other high-vibrating beings and environments, you will actually amplify this energy. That means *you will create even greater highs.*

But let's go further. Let's imagine that we are interacting directly with the universal energy. Let's assume that this energy, which is pure creation, has a very high rate of vibration. Let's go further to say that we are bringing our low vibrational energy to the universe in our depressed state. What's going to happen then? *Nothing.* We are going to cancel each other out so that a big fat nothing happens. We're not creating anything. We're not hearing lovely music at all. We are creating a "no sound region."

The signals (frequencies) that we send out tend to bring us what we're truly asking for—but on a *vibrational* level. This means that what you want may not be what you're expressing energetically. It doesn't matter what your mouth says—if your energy is saying something different, that's what the universe has to create with.

Music is created when sound waves consist of frequencies that have a mathematical relationship. The interference created by meeting and merging sound waves generally creates a resultant wave that contains a discernible and repeating pattern. We find these patterns pleasant. They are normally simple ratios between frequencies, such as 1:1 (unison), 2:1 (octave), 3:2 (perfect fifth), 4:3 (perfect fourth), 5:4 (major third), and 6:5 (minor third).

Dissonance is often the result of sound waves that meet and merge but produce no discernible simple mathematical relationship or repeating pattern.

So, how do we create pleasant-sounding music with the universe (higher energy experiences)? How do we tune our own instrument (our bodies, our thoughts, our deeds) in order to amplify the higher vibrational rate of the things around us, creating more, pulling more to us rather than creating less, or pushing things apart? Add to this what we have already learned about our innate desire to entrain. Another way to think about entrainment is to consider the concept of *sympathetic vibration.* If we picture our guitar again, with the plucked string, we can also see that the strings next to it might be vibrating slightly. That is a sympathetic vibration. When a piece of music plays, and we tap our foot, we are connecting with the sounds in our environment. In a sense, this is also a sympathetic vibration. If you are in a foul mood, and slinging it in my direction, it's quite likely I will also suddenly be in a foul mood. Why? You guessed it. *Sympathetic vibration.*

If we consider the "sounds in our environment" from a perspective of energetic frequency, we might ask ourselves whether we are connecting with sounds that bring us down or sounds that uplift us.

We already know that we have the power to influence our mood by consciously directing ourselves to connect with music that leaves us feeling uplifted rather than depressed. By doing so, we are actually changing our own rate of vibration—which then impacts our environment and possibly even the people around us, who are entraining as well.

In addition to valuable exercises, such as using music itself to directly impact our rate of vibration, we can also practice the following:

- *Detoxify your body.* Toxins in the body slow us down, which is an indication of a lower energy state, meaning lower rate of vibration. Depending on your current state of health, this could mean eating better, drinking less alcohol, quitting smoking, drinking more water, getting more exercise, or limiting your intake of anything that ultimately leaves you feeling sluggish and unwell.

- *Take a look at your environment.* Since we've learned that the energy state of the things around us impacts the resultant state created, it stands to reason that if we are surrounding ourselves with fundamentally negative and low-energy people, we are going to be "entraining" with that state, amplifying it with our own low energy, or—at best—simply cancelling out the energies at work, meaning we're not creating anything. There's that "no sound region." It may also be the case that YOU are helping to create a low or "no sound region" for other people. Yikes!

- *Practice awareness, meditation, anything that allows you to take time out and center yourself.* Becoming aware of your thoughts is critical here. The more negative our thoughts tend to be, the more we pull ourselves down into low energy states. The more we're able to let go of labeling thoughts, the greater release we're able to achieve. Imagine all of that feeling bad (and then feeling bad about feeling bad) as a weight holding you down. By letting it go, you can feel yourself getting lighter. Deep breathing or even yoga breathing (pranayama) can help us to release toxins and increase the flow of oxygen, which also serves to increase energy. If you find it difficult to release the negative thoughts, try simply permitting yourself to witness them without getting worked up about it. (*Yes. Here's me feeling like shit about everything.*) Eventually, this state will move on to something else.

- *Serve others.* When we are in service to others, we are actually raising our level of vibration. When you know that you have helped someone else, it brings with it a very positive feeling. This is uplifting. Conversely, try not to do terrible things or think terrible thoughts about people. This will drag *you* down.

- *Listen to music that is uplifting.* The chapter titled "Kill Your Radio" discusses the benefit of pleasurable music and its impact on our brains. We can, quite literally, impact our brains with sound. Consider playing an instrument. Sing. Chant with a singing bowl. Explore working with tuning forks to impact your "frequencies." It's cool, even if it sounds weird.

- *Spend time communing with nature.* Go outside, sit down somewhere beautiful, and contemplate the unseen forces at work. The connections between everything are really quite miraculous, and while it may currently feel like we're just floating in nothing, it is also quite possible that we are being subtly upheld, at all times, *by everything.*

Things happen in our lives over which we have no control. We get caught up in trying to understand *why* they happened. We get caught up trying to understand why something else is *not* happening. But neither one is relevant. It is what we MAKE from the event that matters…or that MAKES matter. This "terrible" and "unfair" thing happened to you. Now, how can you use it? How can you manipulate your own energy in order to create something incredible from it? This energy is the raw material you need to fashion the stuff of your life.

If life is a concert, then the things that happen to us aren't about paying the price for our tickets just so we can see the show. It isn't about sitting back and waiting to hear something nice so that we can be transported. We are not members of the audience.

We are members of the orchestra.

CHAPTER 16
Loneliness in an Overpopulated World

ORCHESTRA, RIGHT? THAT'S a lot of people, and yet, how is it that you are sitting here all alone? It really doesn't seem like anyone is playing anything with you, which makes it harder to imagine creating beautiful music with the universe. The universe is just one big old empty house when you come home from work or from being out with friends. S P A C E. It's mocking you from your empty bed. You wonder how is it that with 7 billion people on the planet, you are eating your dinner in front of the TV alone again. (And no, the dog and cat don't count in this instance, because let's face it—it's hard to have a meaningful conversation with them.)

The problem with the loneliness is that it feels eternal in that moment. It feels like a condition that will always afflict you.

"Why does no one want me?" is eventually where this leads. It stands to reason, of course, that if you are alone right now, you will always be alone. It's not true. That's what I'd like to tell you. Everything is transitory. The condition of your relationship was. And this will be, too. Except . . .

I can't tell you *when* exactly this current condition will change. I can't tell you *when* you are going to meet some amazing person who will help you to feel less lonely.

I mean, unless you are a shut-in, the chances are good that you will meet people, make friends, and of course there's family—but a soulmate? I don't know. I don't know how long this present state will last. So, rather than fill your head with the notion that you are merely biding your time until the next big thing comes along, I feel it would be much healthier to ask you this:

Can you learn to love your life the way it is now? Meaning, can you accept your aloneness? Can you make it something positive? Something to cherish? Something that builds you into a strong, independent, and joyful person?

I always thought that my strength came from having a solid understanding of the big picture. To me, this meant knowing, in intimate detail, all the little pieces that make up the larger framework of my life. The big picture is made up of many small elements, and if we can know and examine each one of these elements, then we can understand how they fit into the whole. In knowing this, we can see how things connect—and here is the leap: If we can understand how things connect, then we can *anticipate* how they will connect in the future. This was my concept of strength, this understanding, this ability to make intuitive leaps.

Now, I find that I don't understand much of anything. I don't understand how all of my hard work has gotten me to *this* place, which is a place I don't really want to be (because it involves suffering). Or I'm afraid because I know what I want, but I don't see how to get there (which is someplace that doesn't have any suffering). And I don't see how to get there because everything is so unpredictable. I can only control my feelings (and barely that), so how can I go about creating my big picture if I can't see all the pieces?

This unpredictability drains me. It leaves me feeling weak and uncertain. How can I draw up the plans for my life when I don't know what will happen from one moment to the next—and far worse, when I don't have control over most of the elements that may make up that moment? How can I possibly turn all of this *not knowing* and *lack of control* into a position of strength?

In combat, knowledge is the first and most essential weapon. How can you target the enemy if you don't know *who* that enemy is? How can you target them if you don't know *where* they are?

This line of thinking implies that "strength" is a position we hope to obtain because we are trying to protect ourselves from something. Strength is about fortifying. It is about blocking. It is about withstanding. "Power of resisting force" rather than "vigor of action" or "courage."

We feel weak when we say we are vulnerable. When we're lonely, we're feeling very weakened by it. We're torn between allowing ourselves to feel the vulnerability of our aloneness and fortifying ourselves by closing down. Being open means we are also open to attack. There is an enemy out there somewhere, we think, and if we're not strong enough, they'll huff, and puff, and blow down our house.

Some of us (and we know who we are) try to draw our strength by manipulating others. We might belittle people, criticize, make others feel as if there is something wrong with them, or try to figure out what buttons we can push to get them to do what we want. All the while, we're sucking up their life force like a vampire. Other approaches (such as being passive-aggressive) may be more subtle, but the concept is the same. We are, once again, trying to protect ourselves through fortification, through the power of resisting force. We are pushing so we don't get pushed, trying to find some way to gain control, wearing meanness like body armor and forgoing compassion in lieu of self-righteousness. Or, in our loneliness, we use people. We are starving for attention, and so we get it wherever we think we can—perhaps hurting others in the meantime.

But there is something more to strength, I think, than all this self-protection and vampirism. The Tao Te Ching says, "The supreme good is like water, which nourishes all things without trying to. It is content with the low places that people disdain."

Consider a river. It is completely open. It is completely accepting (you can slip in a stone, a foot, a tree limb, or a rusted-out '67 Chevy). When you look into it, you see only yourself. But it can weather massive boulders down into pebbles. It can displace entire buildings. It can fit itself into the smallest crack. It can find its way around the largest rock, carving a path where no path existed. It refuses nothing. It gives itself completely. That is vigor of action, not power of resisting force.

What if our true strength revealed itself in our ability to open, to accept, to give of ourselves, and to create from the things that come rather than through an act of force? What if we demolished our fortresses? What then? What if we released our desire for a specific outcome, a specific picture, even if that meant accepting our *present state*, which just so happens to be loneliness?

I feel as if I spend a good deal of my energy trying to force things to take shape. I have a picture in mind of what I want, and so I set about trying to make that picture come to life. But at what cost? Sometimes, no matter what you do, the picture doesn't come out right. Life is supplying the pieces, but they don't always fit together in the way you might suppose. Imagine putting together a puzzle where you don't know what the final image is meant to be. You turn things right and left, then try to jam pieces together. You're trying to create the image of a lion because you saw a bit of tawny fur, but in the end, what you really have is Meret Oppenheim's 1936 surrealistic sculpture of a fur-covered teacup.

You can keep trying; you can start over again—and really exert your will this time!—but it might be less painful to consider simply reassessing what it is you're trying to create from what you've been given.

I know how hard this is. We can imagine truly beautiful pictures. We can dream amazing things and tell ourselves the most wonderful stories. They all have happy endings. They all contain true love and heroism. We are courageous in our stories. We are brave knights, warrior goddesses, or damsels being rescued. Our picture is never crooked or dark. We're certainly never lonely or sad. We're never imagining a trailer park and a double-wide; we're picturing the two-story Tudor with a deck. We can chart the course of our life so clearly, and then, when we actually go to travel the path, it turns out completely different. The path in our head didn't have a fire swamp. There weren't any puppy-sized rats.

What is strength, then, if not powering through? If not wrestling with the path, trying to change its direction? And why should we let go of what we want? Isn't this giving up? Isn't this resigning ourselves to our position in life? Feeling as if we can get or deserve no better?

No. This is letting go of trying to *force* what we want using tools that may no longer be applicable to our circumstance. It seems to me that it takes more strength to let go of the picture in our heads than it does to continue to try to force it to take shape—most likely with pieces that will never fit together.

This hurts, I think. The idea of letting go makes me cringe. I want, so badly, for my happy ending. I want to hang my beautiful picture.

I want to puff up with pride and say that my hard work and persever-ance made it happen—against all odds. And why shouldn't I? Certain new age philosophies try to tell us that we can have whatever we want, if only we imagine it hard enough. If only we draw enough mental pictures, or write ourselves a check for a million dollars and really truly *believe* that we're bringing it to us, then there it will be. Magic! So then, if I fail to bring about the picture I want, it is only because I failed to imagine hard enough the pieces I would need in order to cre-ate it? While I think there may be something to this—certainly energy can draw energy—I also think that it is incredibly hard to retract our *focus*. It is hard to release our expectations of *form* because we still have a specific picture in mind. We become very attached to one particular personification of our desires because it may be right in front of us. It is something tangible, something we can touch. It is that specific person we can name. That specific job for which we interviewed. It's easier this way because we can't reach out and touch a concept. But this attachment to a specific form, a specific roadmap, when it comes to the realization of our dreams could be the thing that foils us, each and every time. This could be the thing that keeps us suffering.

We also want strength to be the stance we cultivate so that life doesn't hurt. If I'm strong enough, fortified enough, then that must mean I can keep pain at bay. But I'm strong, *and* I'm hurting. I have to let it wash over me because that's all that I can do. Breathe it in, all this pain. I am in the low places. I don't know what to do anymore to make my picture a reality. I have come to the place of *surrender*. I can only let go of *this specific picture*; I can only see what else I can create from the pieces.

When we pull back, even further, from our individual life por-traits, we see that this is all the BIG PICTURE. We are a part of it, affecting it, creating with it—but we cannot force a single thing. It is completely fluid at each moment. It is never fixed. It is never a puzzle with a set number of pieces, nor an image set in stone. Alternatively, the one destination is always many destinations, and many roads. Nothing is static, but our mindset can make it *seem* static. When this happens, it can appear that there is nothing but darkness, and failure, and futile efforts to achieve our dreams.

I want to believe that strength is in embracing the things that come my way—and that has to include the pain and disappointment as much as the surprising twists that lead me in directions I'd never before considered. Strength is my ability to love, my ability to forgive, and my ability to let go. Strength is in my ability to find beauty in any picture—even the one where I stand alone.

But I can no longer continue to define strength as an ability to deny the reality of my life and the role I play in creating it, or to force others to construct the things I *think* I need. Strength is not my ability to protect myself from pain. The picture is always changing. The pain and joy are always fluctuating, blending together to create something new.

As I've grown up, my prayers have changed. They have gone from, "God, please give me breasts" and "God, please give me enough money to pay my quarter of the rent" and "God, please make so-and-so fall madly in love with me," to things that feel so much more humble.

"Please help me to let go. Please help me to continue to give love. Please help me to be calm and aware. Please give me the strength to accept what comes and to grow."

If I can make peace with myself, if I can be calm, then the picture transforms again into what it truly *Is*—and I will finally be free of fear enough to find it beautiful.

THIRD QUARTER
(MONTHS 7 – 9)

CHAPTER 17

BECOMING YOUR OWN VALENTINE

IT WAS MEANT to be a simple, quick outing to the grocery store. The eve of Valentine's Day, my mind had quite naturally turned to thoughts of flowers and various confections shoved into heart shapes, or little stuffed puppy dogs with huge, unblinking eyes holding hearts bearing sentiments meant to melt away the elastic bindings of a woman's panties. To that end, I knew my local grocery store, north of the Ohio State University campus, was bound to be jam-packed full of restless twenty-something bucks buying unimaginative flower arrangements already half-past their prime and red foil boxes of Russell Stover chocolates along with their standard pizza and Pabst fare. I thought I might buy myself flowers right along with them. I thought I might explore the concept of being my *own* Valentine, and so—

What happened next, I blame entirely on the new multivitamins I was taking. Those little veggie-power-packed puppies were singing in my bloodstream with all the verve and vigor of a Baptist Gospel choir mid-Hallelujah. They were infusing me with better cheer—enough to momentarily *like* the idea of being my own Valentine, and that's what I was thinking as I headed down High Street toward the turn lane that would take me into the Giant Eagle parking lot.

Only my car, in collusion with the vitamins and partially benevolent thoughts of cute little twenty-something love, veered, quite suddenly, into the turn lane several car lengths ahead of my intended destination. It cut quickly across opposing traffic, heading directly into the parking lot of…What?

The Hustler Hollywood Store.

The Hustler Store was a relatively new installment to my little area of town. If it seemed out of place across from a Tim Hortons and belly up to the back of the grocery, that's because it was. Where Tim Hortons encouraged you to "Discover Your Perfect Latte," Hustler implored you to "Get Your Heart On." So why was I suddenly sitting in its parking lot when I'd been happily on my way to get toilet paper and bargain-bin roses?

And why I was getting out of my car and walking through the door?

Entering the store did not cause the earth to tilt on its axis. Brightly lit, clean, tasteful displays of somewhat elegant lingerie all greeted me in a perfectly non-threatening manner. They wanted to ease me into it. *"It's not all bump and grind,"* they wanted me to know. *"There's gonna be a little dinner first. Maybe a little Al Green."*

A woman came from behind the counter to welcome me. She was dressed as if she were a saleswoman at Macy's. She greeted me with the same kind of cheerful efficiency I might find there, too. I mean, for a moment, I thought maybe this *was* Macy's, in the cosmetics department, for instance. Except here, the display in front of me, which held packages of mascara, makeup brushes, and tubes of cherry red lipstick, all proved to be miniature vibrators in disguise. This was not your Magic of Macy's, and Kansas had gone bye-bye.

Ah, how cute, I thought, when I saw the fake lipstick. They were romancing me. Getting me to giggle a little. *"Come on. It's not so bad, right?"* they're saying. Except I know that Larry Flynt was never much for beating around the bush (at least not in the way I'm referring to it here), so clearly I hadn't yet reached the Larry Flynt-inspired part of the store. I was still in the I'm-gonna-fake-yawn-and-then-put-my-arm-around-you gently questing hands of his marketing department. This was just the opening act, the tease of their little neighborhood (not your) mom-and-pop store.

They were also toying with my mind. Someone's psychology degree had yielded a giant banner across the back wall. It said, *"Relax. It's just sex."*

Okay. I mean…they're right. It wasn't so bad. No greasy, nasty guy was eyeballing me from behind the counter with one hand absent from view. The floors weren't suspiciously sticky. I didn't feel like I needed a wig and sunglasses to enter—or gallons of disinfectant and maybe a body condom.

But it was all leading up to something, right? They were coaxing me deeper into their lair with their kinky kitsch, and it all pointed to…yes, here it was, that little section marked by a sign: **Must Be 18 or Older to Enter**. Did I dare to cross that line and turn the corner? What would I find?

Apparently, if I dared to cross that line and turn that corner, what I would find was a man, well-dressed and well-spoken (with a hint of edge detectable via the single, small, and unobtrusive stud in his nose), giving a demonstration of various vibratory devices to a small circle of women.

Completely unexpected. I had not thought the experience would be so…educational. Yet, here was a group of women exclaiming over the various highlights of each device as the man delivered his pitch just as smoothly as if he were standing in a living room selling a vacuum to a housewife. And long gone are the days of…well…objects designed to mirror (with 3x magnification) their real-life counterparts in such a way that *you know* you will have to bury it in the bottom drawer, deep beneath the jumble of socks and underwear so that even *you* don't see it until it's called upon for active duty. This stuff looked like chrome-accented sports cars without wheels—modern art pieces you'd be proud to set on your mantle. No one would be the wiser. And its price? It's going to take a couple of Benjamins to drive that baby home. (No pun intended.) That's not even close to how expensive it gets. This world has come a long way from VHS in cheap cardboard sleeves and unmentionable devices meant to make a good girl blush.

When the salesman, who turned out to be the store manager, was done giving his demonstration, he approached me and asked if there was anything he could help with. The hell you say! *Should I spritz him with holy water?* I thought. Make the sign of the cross in his direction? *No eye contact, buddy!* Why would I want someone's help in a place like this?! Isn't it all fairly self-explanatory? Sheesh. Leave me alone with my mild case of mortification, thank you very much. And can you dim the lights while you're at it? These department store fluorescents are making it too easy for you to see my face.

That's the point, of course. They are doing their best to reduce the embarrassment factor by providing a sense of well-lit normalcy, and avoiding the sales staff is not an option—not if you want to get at the stuff they keep in the cases. Yes, you heard right. *Locked* cases. These are fine jewels, ladies and gentlemen. Precious artifacts. Yes, you *could* pick from the stuff in plastic packaging on the outer edges of paradise, but that'd be your loss. The GOODS are under lock and key. So, you gotta talk to somebody. And yes, they will come and unlock the case; they will take out the item you point to; they will expound upon its finer points (and yes again, the manager was very matter-of-fact and not the least bit squeamish when he told me, "Oh! I didn't tell you the coolest feature! This one has a turbo boost, so at the point of orgasm, you just push this button here…").

Um…excuse me. I blanked out for a minute from the sheer force of the blood rushing to my face. How terribly ingenuous of me to be turning this absolutely comic shade of tomato red. Quick! What's my line?

"Uh, wow. These things sure have come a long way."

Since what? I imagine him thinking. As if I've time-warped here from the fifties when a woman's place might have been in the kitchen, where the closest she might get to the Big "O" would be between the letters B and X in ICE BOX.

Clearly, I was no expert in the realm of adult entertainment. But in the name of further *research*

. . . I allowed the manager to talk me into a purchase. Not the one he *wanted* to sell me (you can get five dresses and a pair of sensible pumps at Penny's for that price, ladies), but still

. . . I found myself…bargaining?

"I hadn't planned on spending that much," I admitted to him, as he showed me some top of the line racecar model with built-in rechargeable batteries you never have to replace. (Actually, I hadn't planned on spending *anything*, since entering this store had been the furthest thing from my mind when I set out on my trek for grocery store sundries.)

"You'd be surprised by the cost savings over time," the manager was saying, "depending on the amount of use it gets. We crunch the numbers," he added. "Calculate these things down to the penny per minute."

Argh! I shook my head, quickly. Let us steer clear of the mathematics behind this delicate engagement, please. Put another way, the only mathematics I was interested in at that moment would be the numbers telling me that, no, I was not dropping one-fourth of my rent money on this pale pink-colored ice cream swirl of rechargeable-battery silicone art. How could I put this to the salesman? "My current investment in batteries would be modest, I assure you." *No, I didn't actually say that out loud.*

"I'd rather you get what you want though," he said, "so, let me see what I can do."

He disappeared, leaving me standing by the locked case, mind-boggled by the fact that I was standing next to a rack of DVDs displaying things that—well, really, you get the picture—and then the manager returned, holding a pamphlet. "This will get you 20% off," he said, "which takes you right back down into your price range. Now," he added, smiling, "what color did you want this in?"

For goodness' sake!

(I'm not telling you what color I got.)

At the checkout, he took it out of the box to test it. "You understand, I'm sure, that we want to make certain it works before you leave."

"Yes, yes, I do," I said, nodding. "And I appreciate that." (This isn't Wal-Mart, folks. You can't just take it back.)

"Would you like a Hustler gift bag," he asked, "or a white bag?"

"It really doesn't mat—the white bag," I told him. After all, in that walk from my car to my house, toting my considerably pared-down Giant Eagle purchase of half-wilted carnations and toilet paper, someone might see the *other* bag—and then I'd have to explain what I'd been thinking.

Wait a minute. I suppose that ought to be obvious....

CHAPTER 18
THE HALL PASS: TEMPTATION FOR INSTANT GRATIFICATION

I'D BEEN THINKING about Sex. Sex. S.E.X.

Only, not quite like this:

Pop Quiz. You are sitting at home on a Tuesday night, nursing your broken heart, when out of the blue an old friend contacts you, inviting you to get together. You agree to meet him at a local club where he's playing. During his set break, he quite calmly informs you that his wife has given him a Hall Pass, and—surprise, surprise—he thought of *you*.

After confirming that this means what you think it means, namely that his wife has given him permission to have sex with another woman, do you

a.   Give him your address and ask, "What day is good for you?"
b.   Slap him in the face and say, "How dare you?"
c.   Gracefully reject his proposal, with a deeper understanding that everyone is simply seeking to love and be loved the same as you.

The answer is C.

I'm pretty sure it's C.

At least, C is what *I* answered when this actually happened to me.

I'd met this man just shy of my eighteenth birthday. Almost immediately, I was captivated! He was smart, creative, spiritual, and attractive. It did not take us long to discover that we were kindred spirits, and eventually we became good friends. Romance did not appear to be in the cards for us (although at one point I deeply wanted it to be), and he later married a lovely woman. They had children and went on to live happily ever after. At least, I'd *assumed* the marriage was happy.

We lost touch over the years, until social networking allowed us the opportunity to play distant voyeur to each other's lives. Pictures of his children and wife showed, for all appearances, a lovely life. It was obvious to me that he loved her. He seemed to be doing well.

So, needless to say, this sudden Hall Pass moment caught me quite by surprise. I was at my most vulnerable when he broke the news. It had been six months since my own breakup, and I was still right in the thick of the heartache. I was quite lonely, and beginning to feel like it might be nice to be touched by another human being again. So this…well…there was a fleeting moment when I considered "Option A." Who better to sleep with than someone to whom I'd once felt very close? Someone I'd always found so attractive? One of the rare people with whom I'd resonated?

But.

Also, someone *married*—"Get Out of Monogamy Free" card or not. Someone married, *with kids*. Someone with a child-sized super-hero backpack in his car, visible from over his shoulder as he leaned against the passenger side door and delivered his "Would you mind terribly if I used you for sex" speech, barely blinking an eye. For God's sake! Well, I mean, if he had been *unmarried and not so clearly in love with his wife*, I might be telling you a different story right now—one that starts with something like, "Depends. How quickly can you get me naked?"

Since that wasn't the case, I did the responsible thing. I begged him *not* to take his wife up on her offer—with me or with anyone. "You love her," I said. "You don't want to do this." And it was true. He didn't. Like me, he was suffering. Love will make you do crazy things sometimes, including acting out. I knew the feeling. There had been countless occasions when I pondered what I might do to get the attention of James. If I could make him worry or make him jealous, maybe that would prove that he cared for me. But I couldn't do it. At least not in any serious way. I loved *him* too much to do anything terrible. At first, I'd only drive around late at night in the hopes that one of those times he'd come home from the bar and I wouldn't be there. Surprise! The woman who is always there is suddenly *not* there. This worked only once. The one time I did manage to be out later than he was, he called me, frantically worried. I felt so bad for making him worry that I promised never to do it again!

Try number two was far more extreme. Close to the end of things, I went out on a movie date with another man. The man was an old friend, and it was *mostly* innocent—but I thought it might wake up James to the fact that some other man might actually want me…you know, if he didn't.

This failed to make a suitable impression, which should have told me everything I needed to know.

What it comes down to is this: It's no use. If you are in love with someone, you have to keep trying to make it work until you realize that trying is changing nothing but your own spirit (usually for the worse). But should you come to the realization that it *is* changing your spirit, then it's time to stop and reassess.

In that moment, my love (the universal, unconditional kind) for my long-time friend-who-was-busy-propositioning-me-for-sex was stronger than ever. My heart felt such compassion for him—and for me. It was a clear reminder that we are all soft and vulnerable, aching to be touched, to be loved—aching to be truly *seen* by the people we love. Even when we have someone, sometimes we still feel very much alone.

There will be moments in life when the best we can do is support others in their time of need—even above our *own* pain and the desire we might have to cover it over with whatever band aid might be present (and offering itself to us).

I know. Disappointing.

CHAPTER 19
DISAPPOINTMENT
DYSMORPHIC DISORDER

LET ME SEE.... Nope, this shit STILL ain't fair.

There's nothing that can be done about it. You're going to be moving on. You're going to have more moments when you are feeling good. Okay, maybe not *good*, but at least *okay*. You're going to redo the bedroom so that it doesn't make you cry every time you look at the bed. I recommend choosing a color scheme he *never* would have approved. I chose lilac. I've never had a lilac anything in my life. But it looked good, and it did not remind me of him—no way, no how. Go ahead and pile forty pillows on the bed, so there's no room for him anyway.

Just as you're enjoying a moment of quiet, he's going to worm his way back into your head. *You are going to miss him.*

Yes. I said it. You are going to miss him. If you say this to others, out loud, they will frown at you. They will furrow their brows in confusion. They may even pretend that you didn't say it so that they don't have to respond. Plus, I guarantee that you will not be able to make sense of it any better than they will. You will ask yourself the following question:

"What, exactly, do I miss?" This is an especially interesting question if there were a lot of things that were no good in the relationship. But the chances are fair that your relationship included quite a bit of positive, too. After all, you fell in love, and now that time has passed, you will find yourself remembering those loving times with a clearer head (as opposed to the head that you had in the immediate aftermath when you were so fueled by chemical explosions that you could think of nothing objectively).

For me, the answer to this question, "What exactly do I miss?" turned out to be his ability to make me laugh, his quick mind, and his amazing creativity. His ability to make me laugh was pretty much on or off. If he wasn't making me cry, he was making me laugh. He had an intelligent, caustic wit, a strange and twisted sense of humor that very much matched my own. We understood each other on that level, and this is part of why I fell in love with him. I thought that as long as we were able to hold on to our humor, we would make it. No matter what, we could get through the rough times—especially if we remembered to laugh at ourselves.

Unfortunately, the dark times were too heavy for our laughter. The ability to laugh at ourselves went right out the window, and without the "wit" part, the "caustic" part became too painful, and my ability to remain open and flexible through good humor dried up in the face of so much one-sided emotion. And there you have it. Things happen. It's not fair. What should have/could have been was not and could not.

Thus, the suffering begins again. "I should be over this by now!" you tell yourself. "Why in the hell am I still thinking about him, let alone MISSING him!" It's infuriating, and worse, it reminds you of all the ways in which life has disappointed you. Some of us suffer from what I call **Disappointment Dysmorphic Disorder**. This is characterized by a malformed sense of disappointment, or an over-blown sense of disappointment that's disproportionate to one's life circumstance. Even *this* circumstance. It still feels as if life has been turned upside down. We're still adjusting to a complete change—possibly even a dramatic paradigm shift. We're still working to wrap our heads around the fact that we're alone, and with no way of knowing how long this state might last. "I can be alone right now as long as I don't think I have to do this forever," I tell myself. But the scary thing is that there are no guarantees. When we're caught in the throes of our great disappointment over how things have turned out, we're blind to the tools and unique gifts that we *do* have…the positive things that are happening in our lives right now—the means we have all been given to accomplish our goals and to *create* a path that we will find fulfilling.

One such primary tool is our ability to learn and adapt. Most of life's happenings are beyond our control, and this sense of power-lessness can skew our perspective; but even as things change, we can *learn* to work with the new circumstance. It may take a little bit of time—and then a little bit MORE time, but every moment of our lives, we have the capacity to learn something new. Our brains are capable of expanding, of making amazing cognitive leaps—we can grow new neural networks, make new connections…our "hard disk space" is organic, ever-changing, beyond what we could hope to fill in a lifetime.

The way you are right now *is not the way you have to be forever.* That means that the way you *feel* right now is also not the way you have to feel forever—it's not even how you have to feel a minute from now. It is your choice. Genetics, hardwiring, conditioning, experiences, and the way you have put it all together have created deep-set channels, like grooves in a record, through which you play your individual song. But you can carve new channels. It *is* possible to re-program. We can develop new techniques for dealing with our feelings and our manner of addressing our problems. It will be difficult—it will take diligence, patience, and practice (the fine-tuning of our instruments). Most likely, we will falter more times than we can count—but it *is* possible to change. We never have to remain stuck. In fact, "stuck" is merely a story we tell ourselves.

So what do you do when those moments arrive? When you are struck out of the blue with sadness, with longing, with missing him so much you feel like you could break down and cry about it in the middle of the street?

Breathe it in. It is okay to miss him. It really is. Say it out loud even. "I miss you. Why? Because you used to make me laugh. Thank you for bringing laughter into my life." And when your brain takes you down a different track, namely the one that starts off with, "Will someone else ever make me laugh again?" be gentle, but be truthful. The chances are pretty good that, in fact, someone *has* recently made you laugh. Lucky you! The same can most likely be said of similar questions, like "Will someone ever love me again?" The answer to that is a resounding yes. (I love you. I know it doesn't count, but still.) Try not to put conditions on it. Try not to classify it. Allow it to come to you in whatever form life wills at this point. But see it. It's there, and be glad for it. It will grow if you give it light and time.

WHILE YOU'RE GIVING it light, you can also spend this time working through that feeling of wanting to hunt him down and punch him, repeatedly, in the face.

It was bound to happen. I'd been going around like the Buddha when it came to the topic of being angry. In fact, I was a little dismayed by my inability to *get* angry. I was still the very soul of understanding. Even after I saw THE PICTURE, I wasn't angry. Heart-mutilated, yes. Angry, no.

That took eight months.

When it hit, it was vicious. It was a punch in the gut that made me want to punch *him* in the gut. And the face. And maybe run over him with his red minivan. I would then break every piece of musical equipment he had, preferably over various parts of his body.

I HATED him. It is really only possible to hate someone you love—or someone to whom you've handed over quite a bit of emotional power. I knew this. I knew that this hate, which felt like a heavy black thing eating away at my heart, was really some sort of critical mass of hurt. It was exploding through my body. What he'd done suddenly seemed unforgiveable. He'd left me alone in this house, which he knew I'd only gotten in the first place because of him. He'd left me alone after promising me that he wanted to be with me, although I'd presented him with the opportunity to choose otherwise. He left me alone in a less-than-safe neighborhood and never bothered to check on my well-being. He never bothered to see if I was still alive after all we'd been through together, after all we'd meant to each other. I mean, what kind of person *does* this stuff, I wondered.

Someone awful. Someone evil. Someone...

Sigh. None of it was true. It was negligent tort all over again. What kind of person does this? Someone with his own hurts and frustrations and wounded bits, that's who. Still, I was angry.

"What am I supposed to do with all this anger?" I asked a sink full of dirty dishes I wanted to smash all over the tile floor. The anger, just sitting there, was dangerous. It would flail out at other people with no warning. It would flail out at *me*. I found myself wanting to drive my car into large, stationary objects at high speed. The anger was just as bad as the grief. Obviously, this wasn't doing me any good.

So, what *do* we do with all of the anger? Some people take it right to the source. These are the people who call up their ex to yell obscenities, or worse, show up where their ex is bound to be in order to cause a scene. These are the people who spew acid into the air, barely aware that everything around them is melting down to nothing as a result.

I was determined to avoid becoming one of those people. Keeping it bottled up obviously wasn't any good, nor was taking it out on innocent bystanders. Buddha said, "Holding on to anger is like grasping a hot coal with the intent of throwing it at someone else; you are the one who gets burned."

Well, yes. I was definitely experiencing the hot-coal-burny thingy. So, how to let it go?

I have heard a number of people claim that this feeling of anger is actually empowering. I tell you this much, I must not be very good at being angry because I definitely didn't feel *empowered* by it. In fact, what I felt was nearly the opposite. I felt like I was holding onto a rope tied to the back of a motorcycle, being dragged down the highway at high speed face first. It was not a pleasant feeling, and I felt weak and out of control in addition to being angry. There was no protection being offered behind it.

All I could think about was what the hell was wrong with me and why, why, why did this have to happen? And if it *did* have to happen, why was I the one being tortured for it, while he got away clean?

Let me tell you, all of these feelings failed in being charitable, equanimous, pragmatic, or especially spiritual. I failed to be kind to myself. The brain-munching zombies were back; I suffered through thoughts that said, *Obviously, I am a defective person. Obviously, I deserve to be alone because I AM alone.* All this craziness just made me that much more angry.

It's exhausting, trying to figure out what you should be doing. The answer is that whatever you are doing is what you should be doing, or it's what you should be doing on your way to what you should be doing—and that is absolutely *no* help when, eight months in, out of nowhere some random event or memory knocks down all your defenses, morphing you into an absolute wreck.

I had no idea why, after eight months, I was furious AND also missing him terribly. I was furious AND broken up over the fact the he might never break down and call me. He had, most likely, done an admirable job of moving on. I was the one with the problem. I was the one dissatisfied by what he had been able to offer me. It was true. The decision was just. Here was further proof. He was having no trouble whatsoever moving on. He was having no trouble not calling me. He had not just lost someone whom he had loved with all of his heart. He had lost someone he kinda liked, most of the time, but wasn't crazy in love with by a long shot. Why did I want someone like that? Why would I mourn someone who was not mourning me?

Because love doesn't make any sense, that's why. If it were rational and reasonable, it would probably be less fun! Also, we might have to find some other impetus for creation (or the explosive expressions of our suffering).

So what do you do with all of this? What do you do when you discover that the tears still come—and they are hot with your fury and your pain, and you don't know why you're still breathing since you are, in fact, the loneliest and now also angriest person in the universe—without much of a purpose other than to cart about misery.

It is an enormous weight to carry, the feeling like you are floundering. The feeling of being rejected or victimized hits to the very core of you. The feeling of being stuck. You think you aren't stuck. You thought you'd moved on from it all only to find out that here you are, stuck again. Here you are, in the worst kind of pain because it's not just about the breakup. Admit it. It's about the fact that you are alone, dealing with all of these feelings. You may also wonder if anyone will ever love you again, or wonder whether *you* will ever love someone again. If you "gave" your heart to this person, it suddenly feels a bit like they walked off with it, and now you want it back—with interest.

Personally, I felt something break inside of me. I felt it happening *during* the relationship. I was spirited, and then, suddenly, I felt the breaking of that spirit. I had been vibrating on at least a moderate level, and then there was that no sound region, which then led to an incredibly low, LOW. There is something especially painful that happens when we give our all only to realize that *giving our all* guarantees us nothing. It's humiliating. It's infuriating. It's also very, very heartbreaking. Recovering from that takes time, abrupt spiritual enlightenment, or someone else (whom you're likely to believe because you're wildly attracted to him) telling you that you are the absolute most awesome thing in the whole wide world and it's a wonder that your ex didn't see it.

I will tell you something: I have neither had someone dripping the honeyed juice of the universe on me, nor have I become enlightened. That leaves me stuck with the "takes time" option, which can be a bit of a drag.

These were the things that helped me through:

1. Be patient and compassionate with yourself. When you feel the angry feelings rising up in you, begin taking deep breaths. Acknowledge what you are feeling. Understand that it will pass. In the meantime, it's okay to feel it.

2. There are some things you cannot change or make happen no matter what you do, no matter how you act out, no matter how much you scream and cry about it. Yes. It feels awful. But by admitting that we can't manipulate or tantrum our way out of it, sometimes, we can experience a kind of release from the pressure to make something happen. Just sit there. You don't have to do anything. Maybe breathe, though. That's good.

3. It is very important that we examine our situation as honestly as possible. In many cases, when we are angry and hurt, we lose sight of the truth of our situation. We also overemphasize

the negative and maybe enjoy a good wallow in self-pity—the "poor me" approach. We embrace the role of a helpless victim. But the reality of our situation must be taken into account. We must take responsibility for where we are in the present moment. We may be angry at this other person for hurting us, for acting in ways that may seem unjust to us, but we had some role to play as well. (We will get more into accountability in Part II.)

4. Examine the situation with a sense of equanimity. Deep down, we all crave the same things: love, peace, and happiness. We all make mistakes, suffer from confusion, get hurt, and hurt others. We are all caught up in our stories, forming attachments and tearing away from them. We are all disappointed. You are angry, but could it be true that the person who has hurt you was just the same as you, in a universal sense? They hurt you in search of the things that you seek for yourself. Again, may we all be free from suffering and the causes of suffering. May we do our best not to inflict our suffering on others.

5. Allow yourself to examine the situation against others to gain perspective or a sense of relativity. There are certainly more serious situations and greater suffering than what you are experiencing. Consider the parent who has lost his or her child in a senseless murder. Consider those who are homeless, or starving, or caught up in a war zone, or those who do not have the basic freedoms and rights, which we often take for granted. Consider those suffering from a terrible illness, disability, disfigurement. Be thankful for what you have. If you are not sure what this is, stop and take inventory. A REAL inventory. Yes, you may be on your own, and maybe you have a pile of bills and not enough money to pay them, but you may also have friends, family, strong hands, a good mind—*yourself*. You're still breathing. Put one foot in front of the other. Do the best you can do.

But I am going to stress again the possible benefits of that very first exercise, as it's the one that helped me the most right in the heat of the moment, when I was too mad to think properly or be rational about anything.

STOP

TAKE DEEP BREATHS
When we're angry, we start to breathe from our chests, in short, shallow breaths.

BE PATIENT AND COMPASSIONATE WITH YOURSELF.
Acknowledge what you are feeling. Understand that it will pass. In the meantime, it's okay to feel it.

You could also chant a nursery rhyme, if that works better for you. Quote dialogue from *The Big Lebowski*. Focus in on the details of your surroundings. Sounds. Colors. Shapes. Whatever helps to move you toward a place of calm presence. Anger is considered a destructive force rather than a creative or constructive force. When we're angry, we are thinking mainly about all of the things we have lost or that have been taken from us. At its heart is typically *fear*. Perhaps we think that, if we release our anger, it may leave us weak and vulnerable to further loss and pain. Turn your thoughts towards this notion: Forgiveness can be an act of self-transformation.

We seem to live in a culture where revenge is expected, if not celebrated. We have a revenge mentality. The Wrath of God, Old Testament style (even God was said to be a vengeful God). Countries revenge against each other. *If you cross my border, there will be retaliation. If you go against the family, there will be hell to pay.* But now, we're supposed to stop wanting revenge? We're supposed to forgive the person who has trespassed the borders of our hearts?

> "…forgiveness *is* forgiveness. Your forgiveness of another is your own forgiveness; the forgiveness you give is the forgiveness you receive. If you wholeheartedly forgive

your enemy, you may dare hope for your own forgiveness,
for it is one and the same" (Kierkegaard, *Provocations*).

When we extend our forgiveness to others, we are healing our-selves. We are letting go of the hot coal. We must come to the conclu-sion that our very happiness depends on our ability to forgive. Anger is a poison within us. Resentment is a poison. It will eat away at our hearts, killing both the seeds and the fruits of our joy. If all this sounds a little too poetic for you, let me put it another way:

If you do not forgive and move past your anger and resentment, it will harm you. Maybe it's that heart attack a few years down the road. It's that liver disease you've been courting with the drinking binges. It's that blood pressure that keeps getting higher. Can you die of anger and sadness? Yep. They just don't put that down on the medical charts.

THERE. IT'S FINALLY happened. The road upon which you are walking is branching out into other roads. You have no idea what lies in either direction, all you know is that one of these forks is going to take you...uh...*someplace.*

Personally, I'm not a fan of crossroads. Either direction is asking me to choose an unknown. The way I see it, only *one* of these forks is going to lead me to awesome; the *other* will lead me directly to shithole, mine-laden wastelands. That's too much pressure. *What happens if I choose the wrong thing?* I think. So, I freeze. I would rather just stand there. At least I know this road (and most of its mines, too).

Naturally, I wouldn't mind having things a little more (completely) mapped out. My Magic GPS will direct me to the road where tiny unicorns prance and stones are made of marshmallow moons. But, nope. Reality is erratic. Surprising. Elegant. We will never earn a respite from all of the things in our lives encouraging us to grow, pushing us to make difficult choices or to strengthen our resolve. There is always something demanding more of us—demanding more of our authentic selves. What is this authentic self? I believe it is the part of us that knows our true capabilities. It knows the desires of our heart, and the strength of our spirit—and life is going to keep offering us the opportunity to get it right (even if it just so happens to kill us in the meantime).

So, let's say you find yourself at a crossroads, and you make a choice. I'm no psychic, but I can predict that the result of that choice will most likely *not* be what you had in mind. But try having nothing in mind. It's hard work! Little bits of intention and expectation mix in with our decisions like little bits of Brussels sprouts in otherwise delicious doughnuts. So, assuming that what you encounter on this new path will probably fail to be what you intended, then is there anything you *can* count on?

Perhaps.

This path may lead you to a greater understanding of yourself.

Every choice brings us closer to knowing our own hearts. Every event in life that offers us this opportunity may simply be a means to that end. *What road will show me, ME?*

All of them. Any of them.

Because the truth is probably much closer to the idea that there is *no* path populated solely by tiny prancing unicorns and *no* path populated solely by shithole, mine-laden wastelands. It's both. Dark and light. Shit and unicorns.

That means I have learned enough to say that I have absolutely no idea what any new road will bring. It could be awful, true. And then that awful could turn beautiful. (Beautiawful.) Or I have made a choice, and it appears to be the wrong one. But is it ever? Is that even possible? Can I actually walk down the wrong road? I don't think so, no matter what it looks like.

Sure, no one likes it when "bad" things happen, and I'm not yet advanced enough to feel like falling into gaping holes is a great thing (which is maybe why I keep getting opportunities to fall in them). I want to make perfect decisions with my eyes wide open and my justifications lined up in neat little rows. I want to feel like I have my facts straight. I am always doing the absolute best thing for my future—hell, maybe even for the future of others! I should congratulate myself on being so noble! I am making wise choices here, picking the path that makes the most sense based on solid facts and reasoning and rationalization.

But it's all a sort of spell we weave, magic dust we sprinkle over our heads in order to feel better about the things we do—or to make up for all the messy things we do because we're human and can't help that being human is muddy business and "solid facts" and "reasoning" have a way of falling by the wayside every now and then, as they rightly should. Besides, we have no real way of knowing that we are doing the "best" thing for our future, no matter how righteous we try to be (or think we *ought* to be) in our choices. The reason is because we cannot see the end. We cannot see the final act of this play (I mean, the part before it's curtains). Life happens, and then we get busy sorting it out in our heads (usually in ways that are all wrong and cause a lot of suffering, but hey...when you're good at something...).

Given this, how do I feel about making choices that scare me? Or making choices that push me so far outside my safety zone I might as well be skipping through these mine fields wearing clown shoes? And what about all those choices that seem to just make themselves?

Ask me again tomorrow when I'm one step closer to hacking my way through the carnivorous plant life growing along the edges of this...oh, wait...I mean to say, *I feel excited.*

Right?

It's inevitable. There will come a moment when it hits you… maybe on a Friday night when you are alone. Alone! Going. To. Waste. All that damngoodness. That's right. You've gained back the weight you lost when you were together (because he was sucking the life from you), or you've lost the weight you gained when heartbreak led you on too many dates with Papa John. You have seriously found yourself getting dressed up for the take-out delivery boy and casting long looks at the grocery checkout clerk, fluttering your eyelashes at that delicious man who stocks the fruit at your local co-op. You even briefly considered asking for the phone number of the guy who knocked on your door to see whether you were a registered voter. This kind of hunger makes it seem like God has made you the butt of a cosmic dirty joke.

This is a new kind of misery. The clock is ticking. You can feel it strongly now. Women are made to feel, early in life, as if they have an expiration date. Once we cross a certain threshold, spinsterhood becomes a very real possibility. We know what happens next: all those cats, fuzzy pink sweaters, plus bunny slippers. The specter looms large.

I had every intention of being married by now. I know very few single women my age who, if not already married with children, do not have at least one divorce under their belts. I mean, divorce is terrible, but I look at it this way: At some point, there was a man who actually *wanted* to marry her. For me to be approaching my thirty-sixth year without one single man having proposed either meant that I was simply the most dreadful woman alive or…

Or…

What?

The fates clearly had something else in mind for me. What could it be? If I am being unreasonable when I say I am going to waste, then WHAT? What can be said instead? What is the meaning of all this loveliness sharing space with only my dog and cat (who don't care one way or the other if I put on makeup and comb my hair)?

Answer: *Now is a great time for reflection and healing.*

Fantastic. Only I *have reflected!* I've reflected for eight months now. As for healing, well…okay, you've got me there. I'm still a bit (LOT) raw and vulnerable and yes, I suppose it would be accurate to say that I don't LOVE my life just yet because it still feels incomplete. It still feels like I'm biding time until my *real* life starts. You know, the one where I have a partner who adores me.

What does it mean, exactly, this "going to waste"? Is it like leaving half of a roast beef sandwich in the fridge and then going ahead and buying another one? Is it opening a new package of cookies before the old ones are finished? Something is just sitting around, not getting used for its intended purpose. So what exactly is that intended purpose? Being some man's wife? Becoming a possession? Making sure there are enough clean towels? Learning how to properly fade into the background and change all my opinions to *his* opinions? All right, so that's a worst-case scenario. That's possibly a *bad* marriage, but is this what I mean when I say I am going to waste?

No. It's not.

What I really mean is that I am still an attractive, intelligent, and reasonably witty woman. I am not dead, thank you. I have a pulse. I have woman parts that really like associating with man parts. It would be nice to be favorably reflected in the eyes of someone else. It would be nice to share my life with someone. It would be nice to be valued.

But maybe *that's* not even what I really mean. I have always been the kind of woman who feels like a true partnership can ACTIVATE us. It can make us feel empowered, more ourselves. As if all that resonating we do with that special someone AMPLIFIES our gifts, allowing us to share them with greater reach and impact. That, to me, is what partnership is about. Not a bunch of rules on possession and expectations trying to get other people to provide us with what we lack and also take out the trash and wash the dishes while they're at it.

Yes, I want to be desired again. I want to be valued again. I want to feel the giddiness of falling in love and being loved in return. (That yummy chemical rush!) But this should have nothing to do with whether or not I am *fulfilling my purpose as a woman*. The institution of marriage is not the end-all be-all. To be married is not my purpose as a woman. This is not the 1950s. As a woman, I can create a lot more than a pot roast and babies. Right now, I am creating far more on my own than I'd created in my relationship with James. I am writing more, working more, creating friendships, becoming part of a community that is important to me...I am no longer in a "no sound region." (And that "no sound" region was pretty far from what I had in mind when I was thinking about amplification.) In that case, it's actually better to be on my own than it is to be muted by a "partner."

But there is no intimacy, and I am sorely missing the rush of sharing my damngoodness with someone who can appreciate all facets of it—and that includes sex.

For those of us who tie our hearts and bodies together, meaning frivolous one night stands are out of the question, this can be a challenge. We are suddenly living the life of celibates, and yet we did not sign up to join a nunnery. It can get uncomfortable! Human beings need to touch one another. Unfortunately, some of us have requirements that may rule out sex with drunken strangers, or the guy you saw that one time at Lowe's, whom you briefly considered attacking—like a starving grizzly bear—in the aisle where they stock the furnace filters.

I understand, though, that at some point, you might give up—or rather, give *in* to the temptation to connect with someone you barely know, or with an ex (not *the* ex, but perhaps an older ex) with whom you've remained friends, or maybe even just a friend who's being kind enough to offer his...uh...services, you know, if you get too lonely. (What are friends, for, right?) If this happens, great! Lucky! *There's absolutely no need to feel bad about it.* But if opportunities simply aren't presenting themselves, then you must console yourself with the following—

Treat your body as if it were a thing beloved. Imagine the way you would treat it if you were preparing to meet a lover. See it through the eyes of someone who would cherish it. This means, cherish it yourself. I know it may seem like a poor substitute, but the more radiant you become, the more you adore *yourself*, the more this lovely energy will radiate out into the world, attracting others (and that's not supposed to be the goal, but hey, it's a nice side effect).

Don't be afraid to BE in your body. There's a great temptation to numb out, to distance yourself from the physical because it seems easier to pretend you don't have needs. But it's okay to inhabit yourself and this world IN your body. Exercise can sometimes be a good way to do this, physical activities like dancing, biking, running, etc. When I started doing Pilates again, I fell in love with my legs. Seriously, I have excellent legs!

Also, buy a vibrator. Yep. I said it (and did it, obviously). Or whatever works for you. Masturbation is good for you. (No, it doesn't lead to hysteria, epileptic fits, or blindness.) Actually, studies have shown that masturbation can relieve stress, release endorphins that improve your mood, aid in sleep or increase energy, and, for women, lessen the risk of yeast infections and reduce premenstrual cramping. Also, let's face it. It's *very* safe sex—not only physically but also emotionally during this incredibly vulnerable time.

Last but not least, embrace solitude the best that you can. When you are alone—yes, even on a Friday night—take a deep breath. Breathe in the silence. Feel the peace in it. Hear these words in your heart:

I am right where I am supposed to be.

Do you believe me?

These words are true. You are right where you are supposed to be. Every single thing is right where it's supposed to be. What is missing? Nothing! I promise!

There is no ring on your finger. There is no man in your bed. It is unlikely that there is a million-dollar surplus in your bank account. Okay, I mean, the list of things you *do not have* is way too long and ridiculous to keep going on about. It's like listing all the things you are not. (You are not a can of creamed corn. You are not a paperclip.) But what you *do* have is YOU and POSSIBILITIES. You have freedom. You have creativity, and the time and space to use it. You have more opportunity to follow your whims and your bliss and guess what? You don't have to check in. You don't have to tiptoe. You don't have to argue over what movie to watch, what music to listen to, what to have for dinner, what time to go to bed. You don't have to answer to anyone but yourself.

The idea that no one is taking care of you isn't true. I would argue that you are taking better care of yourself now (after the most brutal part of the grief phase has passed) than you were while you were actually in the relationship. Back then, you were splitting your attention, and probably giving up things that were important to you because making him happy became more important to you. Now, unless you have children, it's all you. Which is *also* why I recommend eventually getting a pet or volunteering or doing something service-related, because all that YOU can get a little unhealthy if you don't find a way to exit the cave of your own head and put all this awesome to good use, even if you don't quite have the amplification you were hoping for. In short, Extend. Grow. Use this time. You are *not* going to waste.

I repeat, you are NOT going to waste.

Channel all that desire. Radiate the fire you feel and *warm other people.* Burn out the toxins. You are coming to life again, and the feeling of it in your limbs may, at first, be a bit painful, like the prickly feeling you get when an arm has fallen asleep and begins to wake back up. But life is never wasted when you extend yourself to others. Energy never dies; it simply changes form.

PART II
THE BODHICITTA
OF BREAKING UP

FOURTH QUARTER
(MONTHS 10 – 12)

CHAPTER 23

DARTH VADER AND THE ABSENCE OF GOD

IF THERE WAS one thing I'd learned in the past nine months, it would be this: Love can be a disastrous distraction. I do not say this with the intent to diminish love in the least. I only say this because it is the truth, and we've all experienced it. We've all gotten so caught up that we've forgotten the things that are most important. If lovers actually *were* brought together by some chubby, winged cupid shooting fiery arrows, then imagine if, after the fact, Cupid cared not one whit for the lovers but only for the *product* of that love. What are you doing with such a great and powerful gift?

The goal of some is to start a family—to have children. This is the primary and most tangible product of their love. In fact, this is perhaps the most common form of love's expression. To some degree, our society expects it—and biologically, it does appear to be an imperative. But love can also serve as inspiration for our greatest creations. It can be a tool we use to shape ourselves. Our change in consciousness is the product.

Yet, we are bewitched. We forget about the product. We forget that we'd intended, all along, to *create* something. We are working on a Project. That Project is our selves. We are growing. We are learning and evolving and bringing forth into the world. When we stop, we become stagnant. The things around us begin to grow stale, and shortly after, we may find ourselves experiencing depression, a sense of extreme dissatisfaction with our lives. We may begin to look around us, typically so that we can point the finger and place the blame for our condition. We are not where we wanted to be. We are not who we think we should be. Who is responsible? How can we gain the power to do something about it?

Our relationships can fill us with doubts and uncertainties, which, on the surface, look as if they have to do with the other person. I know mine did! But dig down, dig deep enough, and the truth is that the doubts and insecurities have to do with our relationship to ourselves. They have to do with our relationship to the divine and to the Project we undertake, which is to have something to contribute to society. It is to bring forth the things that are within us and, perhaps if we're lucky, to touch other lives in ways that will be positive and encouraging.

What do I want to cultivate? That has always been the question. I want to cultivate Compassion. I want to cultivate Peace, Acceptance, and Love (the kind of love that is not driven by ego-needs). So, if this is what I want to grow, how do I do it? Am I doing it? What should be my focus?

Love and the loss of it are teaching me this lesson. It is a painful one, but it is also critical. *The things we require most cannot be found within another person.* They must be found within us, or they must be found through God. (When I say "God" here, this is meant to encompass whatever may be your understanding of a Higher Power or Universal energy.)

So, what are these requirements? Foremost among them may be validation. We want to feel as if our lives have value and meaning—that we have a purpose. We are looking for ways to justify the fact that we are alive amidst such awful circumstances. Aside from the conditions of the world at large (hunger, war, poverty, racism, genocide), there are a seemingly infinite number of smaller and far more intimate sufferings, which we must endure as human beings. There is the personal tragedy of our individual life stories—illness, broken homes, economic hardships, abuse. Beyond this, there is personal confusion over the actualization of our dreams, which we may have abandoned entirely or come close to giving up. There is love lost. Family lost. And to make matters worse, there is the ever-present knowledge that our own death lurks in the shadows. We are constantly reminded of it through the frailty of our bodies, or in the odd dichotomy that is both their beauty and their painful unpredictability.

Man has the capacity to dream such intensely wonderful dreams. We can imagine the divine. We can aspire to things that feel beyond this world, yet we are locked in this flesh, which will decay. We are faced with our own impending doom and the impending doom of all that we love.[16]

In this knowledge lies much of our suffering. Why are we here? If we turn away from a belief system through which we try to answer this question, we are left with very little to go on and an incredible weight to shoulder. But even if we believe in God, he is most likely highly mysterious. He does not descend from the clouds and read off for us, from a list, our duty while on this earth plane. Nor does he rustle the leaves to get our attention, and then speak to us in plain words while we're standing on the edge of a mountain. In short, if there is a God, in an anthropomorphic sense, he isn't spelling it out.

But those needs remain: the need to know why we are here; the need to feel as if we are fulfilling some purpose; the need to feel as if our suffering is not in vain, and that there is a reason to continue to wake each day and face our lives. Perhaps we can train ourselves to give up these questions, to which there are certainly no concrete answers. We should continue to cultivate the best qualities within ourselves, to share what it is we have learned, and to aid others in their suffering. That's it. Perhaps this is our greater answer, our deeper meaning. There is only what Is. But this is an infinitely challenging task.

While we are in the process of reconciling our questions with our lack of answers, in our pain we turn to others. In our pain, and in the absence of a higher power, we turn to humans to provide us with the things we lack. In some cases, this goes beyond simple companionship, warmth, and love. This can include the need for validation, the need for spiritual affirmation, or even the need for salvation—the need to be made whole and to be elevated in status through our relationships.

LOVE IN THE ABSENCE OF GOD

Relationships cannot provide for our spiritual deficiencies. Our relationship partners (in all forms of relationship) may serve as mirrors. They may show us ourselves. They may serve as the sharp edges against which we shed what is now outgrown; they may serve as the soft places where we rest when we are deeply wounded and in need of a safe place. All of these things are invaluable. But can we be made "whole" through another human being? Can we truly understand and fully accept our own value as human beings *solely* through relationships with others?

In order to effectuate this, we would need "an object that reflects a truly ideal image of ourselves."[17] But our human partners cannot do this—at least, not consistently and eternally. They see us through their own filters, which means eventually, we become imperfect in their eyes. This is less than the nourishment we seek where we are accepted, loved, and cherished for ourselves, exactly as we are, with no one seeking to change us to fit their molds, or their own needs, or even what they feel would be most healthy and beneficial for us. The only place where we can receive such unwavering compassion and perfect love is from within ourselves and/or from a power we feel is greater than ourselves. Even so, it is difficult to love ourselves in our entirety when so many others are pointing out such brutal failings—perhaps another important function of relationship, which inspires us to become better people.

Still, our frustration grows. What we seek from our relationships is not always what we get. We may become defensive, or we may attack. After all, we must suddenly cut down to size the person to whom we had previously granted such power. Nietzsche, in *Beyond Good and Evil,* said it best: "When we have to change an opinion about anyone, we charge heavily to his account the inconvenience he thereby causes us." We're also suddenly upset that we have not been brought redemption—or put another way, we're upset that our partner has not magically made everything better. Yet we continue to seek the proof of our value in the eyes of others—in their acceptance, in their congratulations, in their accolades, in their response to what we present to the world. (If we don't have a relationship, we may find ourselves seeking validation/redemption through our vocation or job instead.)

So then, what is the product of love? Is it a perfect self? Is it a self that is flawed but found beautiful in the eyes of our partner? Our culture has been inundated with fairy tales that lead us to believe that true love is always harmonious. Our true love will never contradict us. There will be no need to fight. There is never conflict. We do a disservice to ourselves and to our partners when we believe this. When we hold to this notion, I think we're mistaking spiritual love for romantic love. We are mistaking the love a higher power might bear for us (or agápe love) and the love we share with humans, who face the same suffering we face—those whose death is also guaranteed. We serve each other best in our compassion, in our sharing, and in our awareness of our own deeply flawed nature. We love our partners, and we are aware of their imperfections as we witness them. The product is growth. We must first acknowledge our needs and wants, and then we must free our partners from them; we must allow them room for their own growth, and for the fact that the most important thing is *The Project*—the continued work on ourselves, our relationship with Self and with the universe, in order to be of better service to others through whatever means.

In the end, this will only increase our ability to have and sustain positive and productive relationships. By releasing our partners from as many of the overreaching expectations as we can—by allowing them their humanity again, instead of burdening them with tasks far beyond human capability—we bring about the possibility of deep and *realistic* connections, which leaves room for the unexpected and disappointment as well as the chance to practice forgiveness and compassion. By bringing God (or an enhanced awareness of the universe) back into the equation, we allow ourselves to feel again the infinite, the abstract—the sense that there are things beyond our human understanding and that the unknown itself leaves room for joy as much as for pain. We become more willing to accept a state of groundlessness, of not knowing, and of *faith* through spiritual practice than we are through our experience with human relationships alone, where we feel the tug and pull of individuals with specific (often ego-driven) needs and wants.

I realize that I speak here of "God," but again, I do not seek to define It or categorize It. I cannot answer the question of what God is, or what denomination is "best," or what these terms might mean in your own life. I mean only to address the concept of faith, and the idea that we must not lose sight of the product of our relationships—first and foremost the relationship we have with ourselves. We are all connected. These connections can propel us to a greater understanding of ourselves and others or they can tangle us up in knots, making it impossible to grow. When the fear of loss begins to overwhelm us, it is a sure indication that our feelings of love have meshed with something far beyond the person for whom we hold such feelings.

When it comes to examining our relationships, and whether they are helping us to grow or keeping us stagnant, we may find ourselves suddenly terrified of the choices before us. In many cases, we begin to focus solely on the connections we have forged rather than the *quality* of those connections or what we may be *transmitting* via those connections. Not only are we tied to our partners, but we may also find ourselves tied to *their* ties, including family, friends, and community. This means that when we face the notion of severing our link with someone, we're also faced with the difficult task of releasing ourselves from a spaghetti-like tangle of far-reaching links we have been forging over time. This is daunting, for certain. But refusing to disengage from connections that no longer serve our growth or produce something valuable means that we are allowing fear to determine our path. Stagnation is the result. We may feel as if we are honoring the higher good by making a choice that *appears* less likely to hurt others—including ourselves—but this is an arrogant presumption. I would argue that a life that lacks movement and discovery of the needs of our *authentic* self—true growth—fails to be in service to the higher good. It may even be accurate to say that we cannot *truly* be in service to others, even those whom we profess to love, without first discovering our true path. This is the path that makes our heart rejoice—although it may take all the courage we have to walk it.

LETTING GO: THE REDEMPTION OF DARTH VADER

My generation grew up with a very popular series of movies that shed new light on Joseph Campbell's hero's journey. While this was a tale that combined great adventure with classic mythological concepts, subsequent generations also discovered a classic love story. These movies were the *Star Wars* Trilogy and the prequels that followed over a decade later.

The story of Darth Vader (Anakin Skywalker) and his fall to the dark side was also a story about love and fear. Ironically, one might say that Anakin gave up his soul, twisted by the fear of losing his beloved Padmé. The very steps he took to ensure her safety eventually led to her demise…and to the destruction of the values and political ideals, which he and Padmé had fought to protect. The vision of her death, which haunted Anakin, *was one he brought about himself.* His love was grotesquely twisted by his fear and his inability to let go. He could only believe in his own power. He was unable to accept *the unknown.* He was unable to accept his own powerlessness over life and its subsequent loss in death.

One could argue that this was, indeed, also part of his Project. In the end, Darth Vader is redeemed—if not through the very spirit of his children, certainly a tangible product of his love, then through the choices they made, which he could not.

Darth Vader's son, Luke, refused to join forces with the evil Palpatine. When Darth Vader saw Luke suffering as a result of his heroic choice, he sacrificed himself to save his son. He was finally released from the Dark Side through a greater understanding of love and the force it carries when unencumbered by fear. He was freed. There was no longer a need for the mask. His hero's journey was complete.

Our own hero journey may very well be about learning to let go—not only of the things we fear losing the most, but also of the constant struggle to gain what we think we need from others in order to be happy. This struggle leaves us seeking approval, validation, and love from those who enter our lives, and most of our actions—whether consciously or subconsciously—are geared toward acquiring it. We're like baby birds, mouths gaping open, waiting to be fed. The only solution to our dilemma is to learn to feed ourselves. Inevitably, this must lead us to a different path; it must lead us to a deeper place where we seek answers from within ourselves. A spiritual solution to our problems must follow. There is more happening in the universe than what we can readily see—perhaps not because we are too small to see it but because we have forced our vision to too narrow a path. The larger design of our lives may very well be the greatest work of art ever created. But our limited vision leads us to suffer. We are waiting, once again, with our tunnel vision and our need for definitives. We see the path, which has disappeared behind us, and we become lost in our sadness over where it has led. All the while we are immobilized; the unhappiness we feel suffocates us.

> "Thus are we put in training for a love which knows not sex, nor person, nor partiality, but which seeks virtue and wisdom everywhere, to the end of increasing virtue and wisdom. We are by nature observers, and thereby learners. That is our permanent state. But we are often made to feel that our affections are but tents of a night. Though slowly and with pain, the objects of the affections change, as the objects of thought do. There are moments when the affections rule and absorb the man and make his happiness dependent on a person or persons. But in health the mind is presently seen again—its overarching vault, bright with galaxies of immutable lights, and the warm loves and fears that swept over us as clouds must lose their finite character and blend with God, to attain their own perfection. But we need not fear that we can lose any thing by the progress of the soul. The soul may be trusted to the end. That which is so beautiful and attractive as these relations, must be succeeded and supplanted only by what is more beautiful, and so on forever" (Ralph Waldo Emmerson, From *Essays: First Series*; Essay 5, 1841).

There is still a chance for redemption. There is still a chance to remove "the mask" and the armor we wear, which is meant to cover the ways in which we are damaged more than it is meant to protect us. When Luke asks Yoda what is in the dark cave on Dagobah, Yoda tells him, "Only what you take with you." Freidrich Nietzsche said, "In the end one only experiences oneself." Thus, we begin to see that the most important journey we take is the one that leads within and then *back out again*. When we are able to face our own dark side, to resolve the fear that sits in our hearts, we are able to open to love again—and to forge a new path.

IN BUDDHISM, BODHICITTA is the intention to achieve Buddhahood as quickly as possible, so that one may benefit sentient beings. If the achievement of Buddhahood seems too lofty a goal in this moment, consider that it also refers to the aim of bringing happiness to others and to relieve them of suffering. This could be considered the seeking of enlightenment.

In Sanskrit, "Bodhi" means *awakening* or *enlightenment*. "Citta" denotes *that which is conscious,* so "Bodhicitta" is often translated to mean *awakening mind* or *mind of enlightenment.*

Yet another definition of bodhicitta is the union of compassion and wisdom. The aim is to develop limitless compassion for all beings and to experience or strive for the release of attachments to the illusion of an inherently existent self.

So, to this end, how do we achieve bodhicitta in our breakup?

The first step in any practice is the contemplation of what are called the Four Immeasurables. These are as follows:

1. **Loving Kindness Toward All:** the hope that a person will be well

2. **Compassion:** the hope that a person's suffering will diminish

3. **Empathetic Joy**: taking joy in the accomplishments of others

4. **Equanimity:** learning to accept loss and gain, praise and blame, and success and failure all with detachment, equally for oneself and for others

Let's examine each of these elements more closely.

LOVING KINDNESS AND COMPASSION

Loving kindness and compassion towards all includes the person who just thoroughly hurt you or broke your heart. This is cultivating the hope that he will be well. I know. It seems like a very tall order. It might also seem like an *impossible* order. Most likely, once you hit the anger phase, you will be feeling neither love nor kindness toward your ex-partner. In addition, I doubt that in every moment of the day, you are wishing him well. You may *want* to wish him well, and in certain lucid moments, you may even mouth the words, but mainly you will want to see him suffer. You hope that he's miserable. That his new woman is nothing like he imagined. That his toes develop gangrene, and that an Alien Facehugger enters his room one night and implants one of those chest bursters inside of him.

Unfortunately, this is not the path toward peace.

The first step in cultivating loving-kindness is to direct it to yourself. (You know, you have to put the oxygen mask on yourself first in the event of a plane crash before you can be of any help to others.) During this period of intense suffering, the chances are pretty good that you are not being very nice to YOU. Your self-esteem may be suffering. You may be wondering what is wrong with you—too much of one thing, not enough of something else. You may be mistreating your body, pouring in chemicals, not feeding it well, not exercising, not giving it enough sleep. In general, your broken heart and subsequent numbness impacts not only the way you feel about him and everyone else but also the way you feel about YOU. Love is suddenly in very short supply, when of course you need it most.

One method that is common to Buddhist practice is to train with slogans. This can be a specific slogan (of which there are traditionally 59, called Lojong) or any phrase you find that resonates with you and is positive—anything to disrupt the negative tape that is playing over and over in your head. As I've noted before, the prayer I found to be most helpful was, *May I be free from suffering and the causes of suffering.*

Next, we introduce the practice of Tonglen. This is the Tibetan practice of "giving and taking" or "sending and receiving." It is a meditation practice whereby one visualizes oneself taking in the suffering of others on the in-breath and sending out peace and love to all beings on the out-breath. This practice is typically done in stages, where we first focus our efforts on someone close to us—a good friend or beloved family member. That shouldn't be too difficult, right? Consider someone upon whom you may have recently come to rely, the person to whom you've been spilling your guts, for instance. Surely you can muster up some loving kindness for them, since they are probably suffering as a result of putting up with *your* suffering.

One way we can practice this would be to say,

May [friend's name] *be free of suffering and the causes of suffering.*

On the in-breath, picture yourself taking in their suffering. On the out-breath, picture yourself sending out peace and love.

You may think here about what their life is like. You know it's not perfect. All this time you are crying to them, but most certainly in the meantime, they are experiencing their own troubles. Perhaps their own relationship is on rocky ground, or their health is in decline. They may be having trouble at work. Whatever it is, direct your thoughts toward them; take in their suffering as your own. Wish for them to be free of their pain.

Once you have practiced this for a while, it is time to move on to something a little harder.

Pick someone neutral. Someone you might see every day but who brings up no strong feelings in either the negative or the positive. Direct your loving-kindness practice toward this person, and whatever he or she might be going through.

May [neutral name] *be free of suffering and the causes of suffering.*

Since you may not know this person well, you may be unable to picture the specific events happening in his or her life that might bring suffering, but you can still imagine yourself taking it in and sending back out peace and love.

Finally, this brings us to the practice of sending and receiving with a difficult person. That would be someone toward whom we *do* hold negative feelings. In this case, we're going to practice with our ex, and "difficult" might be putting it mildly.

We are going to sit there, knowing full well that this person suffers because most likely, we had a rather intimate view of it. We were a part of his life, and we knew his challenges—perhaps he had issues with his family and responsibilities. Perhaps he suffered health-wise or had challenges with his career. Whatever it is, we were once very close to it. We had a front row seat, and now is the time to recall that we felt compassion and sympathy for it at some point during our time with him. We wanted to help. We wanted to extend our arms and do whatever we could to ease his pain. And now, although we are no longer intimately involved with his life, we can still offer our support and compassion. We can sit here right now and wish him to be free of suffering in the same way that WE so desperately want to be free of it. In wishing him to be free, fully, in our hearts, we move ourselves that much closer to being free ourselves.

May [name of ex] *be free of suffering and the causes of suffering.*

Picture yourself taking in his suffering on the in-breath. On the out-breath, send him peace and love.

Once you are able to do this, the idea is to include the world, "All sentient beings" in our hopes and wishes for the freedom of others.

Now, rinse. Repeat.

It may take a while for it to be sincere. Sometimes, it may take a *long* while. But consider this: "The good man's love ends in love; the bad man's love, in hate" (Kshemendra's Kalpalata). Once you really catch a glimpse of how everyone, in their suffering, is much like you, it should become difficult to withhold compassion and love, even to those who are…"difficult."

Mudita: Empathetic Joy

Imagine yourself as a parent watching your child score the winning goal. Or they just won a spelling bee. They painted a picture you will hang on the fridge, made you an awesome necklace out of macaroni, or they just won the Nobel Peace Prize. In short, they have done something amazing, and you are proud and joyful. You feel happiness purely as a result of another's joy and accomplishments.

Now, imagine feeling this way for your ex-partner. Yes. I know. Hard to imagine.

For instance, in my case, I know James has found someone else—someone he once loved, in fact. This means that he will not be alone. He will not have to suffer this breakup on his own or be lonely. His friends will rally behind him. There is the chance that this woman will be an excellent match for him—and he will find much happiness in his life with her.

It is so easy for this thought to bring anger instead of joy. It's easy for this to bring feelings of bitterness, but then I am reminded not only of the practice of wanting others (myself included) to be free of suffering but now also this: Mudita, which translates from Sanskrit into "joy," and specifically refers to sympathetic or vicarious joy, which we might find from delighting in the well-being and accomplishments of others *rather than begrudging them.*

Yes. This is more difficult practice. It is one thing to wish that our enemies be free from suffering, but to take the additional step of rejoicing in their happiness when we might be suffering ourselves still feels unfair. We may envy their position. We may covet what they have. This then leads us down the road of comparing our life with theirs and what we feel we lack. Empathetic joy gives way quite easily to self-pity. *I can't be happy for you because look at my own miserable life! Especially YOU don't deserve it compared to ME. I mean, look what I did* **for** *you, and look what you did* **to** *me!*

So, how do we do it? What's the secret?

First, it is easier to feel joy for others when we are feeling joy ourselves. Imagine again the scenario in which your ex-partner has found someone new. They are in love and intensely happy. Now, imagine that you, too, have found the love of your life. He is perfect for you, and you are feeling intense joy. Notice how much easier it would then be for you to feel glad for your ex, and glad for what happened? After all, you might not have met this new person and developed this incredible new life if it weren't for what happened in your past relationships. You are happy, and so why now begrudge the other person his happiness?

Clearly you were meant to part ways so that you could both move on and grow in new directions.

Now, back to the present. (Ugh. I know. I was excited to have met my soulmate in that fantasy, too.) Consider acting *as if*. That doesn't necessarily mean you must act as if you have found the love of your life, but rather the result—the knowledge you gain that you were meant to part ways to create space for something different. Beyond that, there is the knowledge that the person you are now and will become has been shaped by all the events leading up to this moment. It is your choice as to how you allow them to shape you. In your new life, there are things for which to be grateful. If, at this time, you can't find the joy in your own life, be happy for the joy in the lives others; but *also know this:*

If you can be happy for the joy in the lives of others, *you will find more joy in your own life.* Isn't that neat? That means that instead of telling you that you first need to work on finding joy in your own life so that you can be happy for others, I'm saying, concentrate on the reverse. Be so incredibly happy for others! Things are going well for them! They are happy! You want them to be happy. You want to contribute to their happiness. It's much easier this way. Trying to wring joy out of your own life right now might feel a bit like trying to wring sweet Napa Valley wine out of a rotten turnip.

EQUANIMITY

Equanimity can be defined as "Mental calmness, composure, and evenness of temper, especially in a difficult situation." When I talk about having equanimity, I am talking about an ability to experience impartiality—not to be mistaken for indifference or lack of caring. This is letting go of our constant vacillation between good and bad—attraction and repulsion. With equanimity, all things become equal.

Without equanimity, we will constantly find ourselves being pulled in every direction by our mind and emotions. Things become good. Things become bad. But reality tells us time and time again that our judgment in such matters, when taken over a long time, is often hasty.

Consider the following popular Zen parable about a Chinese farmer.[18]

Who Knows What's Good or Bad? A Story

In ancient China, there lived an old farmer who worked a small plot of land with his teenage son. They were poor even by the most modest standards. During this time, horses were considered great treasures; the richest person in the province owned no more than a few of them. One day, a wild horse came galloping into the town, jumped the old farmer's fence, and began grazing on his land. According to local law, this meant that the horse now rightfully belonged to him and his family. The boy could hardly contain his joy, but the father put his hand on his son's shoulder and said, "Who knows if this is good or bad? We shall see."

The next day, the horse made its escape back to the mountains, and the boy was heartbroken. "Who knows if this is good or bad? We shall see," said his father again, with the same equanimity he'd shown the day before. On the third day, the horse returned with a dozen wild horses following! The boy could hardly believe his good fortune. "We're rich!" he cried, to which the father replied, "Who knows if this is good or bad? We shall see." On the fourth day, the boy climbed on one of the wild horses and was thrown, breaking his leg when he landed. His father ran to get the doctor and was soon helping him treat the boy, who was crying and complaining about his miserable fate. The old farmer wiped the boy's forehead with a wet cloth, looked deeply into his eyes, and said directly, "My dear son, who knows if this is good or bad? We shall see." And on the fifth day, the province went to war, and army recruiters came through the town and conscripted all the young men—except for the one with a broken leg.

This story suggests that we may never know the full significance an event will have in our lives. We are so busy labeling everything, stamping it with Good or Bad so that we will know how to react and feel that we can't allow ourselves to stop and simply let go of labels altogether. It is neither good nor bad. It simply IS. It is equal. We can look upon it with impartiality. Whatever happens, fine.

Thus, we meet the man of our dreams. We are deliriously happy and label it Good. We went through so much before—all to get to this Good thing. Like a reward! And then? Well, he has broken our heart, hasn't he? And this is Bad. We are very sad now, and life has let us down because it seemed like we were due for good things. So now, we are being punished.

But of course, this is all ridiculous and never-ending. The only solution to getting off the merry-go-round is to stop labeling, stop feeling the need to name everything. Most of the time, the things we name don't care what we've named them. It changes them not one bit! Some things are. Some things are not. Some things come. Some things go. Buddhists have a slogan for this: "Be patient whichever of the two occurs." Whatever happens, maintain equanimity. Be patient. When it is good, this, too, shall pass. When it is bad, this, too, shall pass.

GESHE CHEKHAWA, THE great Buddhist meditation master and author of *Training the Mind in Seven Points,* suggests that we should train ourselves "with the verses during all activities." He was referring to the Root Verses of the Seven Point Mind Training, which is a set of (approximately 59) aphorisms developed to help train the mind. These aphorisms, or slogans, are meant to be used as an "antidote" to unhealthy mental habits. Essentially, they are tools to help us "tame" the mind, which has, on many occasions, been likened to a wild horse. It runs wild; rears up with barely any provocation; it may throw us from its back and then, if we're not careful, we'll be trampled by it. Taming it is a challenge, to say the least. Once the mind is off and running, it's hard to coax it back into the barn!

The following is a selection of slogans taken from Geshe Chekhawa's *Root Verses of the Seven Point Mind Training* (1102–1176)[19], along with my suggestions for ways they may be applied as an "antidote" to aid us in our recovery.

"CONSIDER PHENOMENA TO BE LIKE A DREAM"

The ground beneath our feet is far less substantial than we might imagine. In a sense, we could say that all things are illusion…and in this, I am not talking about the furniture that you're sitting on, or this book in your hands, but the thoughts that we draw from the things around us. The stories that we tell ourselves about those things. Life is always shifting. We may not have the power to change an event, but we do have the power to change our perspective. We can see something new simply by changing the way we look at it.

Is it an E, M, W, or 3? Depends on how you look at it!

In this way, we begin to see that it is really the names we give to things, and not the things themselves, that can lead us into suffering. We are interconnected in ways we can barely imagine, and yet our minds insist upon something different. What we see as solid is a field generated by the excited vibration of atoms. The only constant is change. We have just experienced this on a very personal level, and yet we resist because change is so uncomfortable. Life has just taken an extreme turn, and the foundation upon which we were standing has shifted, leaving us feeling like we are nowhere. We want to hold tight to everything in our lives, but this is like wanting to hold tight to vapor, or as Alan Watts would say, "...trying to get the water of life into neat and permanent packages." It cannot be done. All this futility seems so frustrating, so sad, but that is just another story, just a dream.

"ANALYZE THE NATURE OF UN-GENERATED AWARENESS"

This is tricky, and it can be a little scary. Have you ever had a moment where everything seems to dissolve? Look at a tree on a sunny day, at the way the sun shines through the leaves. Consider how amazing that tree is—everything it takes to make just that one tree. It's so beautiful! Can you imagine making something like that yourself? Creating a seed that grows into such a thing—something that can provide food, shelter, cleaner air, shade? Marvel at its very existence. What's more, *you* are standing there looking at it. You are formulating thoughts and feelings about it. What ARE you? You are a human being, a conscious human being, on planet Earth, in the Milky Way Galaxy. You are AWARE of yourself. You can ask, "Who is this that asks?" You are aware of your awareness. How is it that you are here? Truly consider it. How is it that you came to be in this place, standing there, looking at this tree? How did humans come to be? How is it that this beautiful tree is here with you?

Perhaps you believe in a God that created all of mankind in seven days. Perhaps you believe that we evolved out of cosmic soup. Perhaps you believe that the world is sitting on the backs of giant turtles. Whatever your belief, put yourself in a place of stillness and draw your awareness as far back as you can take it. You are standing there, looking at a tree. Move your awareness up the trunk of that tree, up further to the sky, up further to the stars in space, and further out, to the galaxy encompassing all of this. Everything is revolving, spinning within a larger orbit. When you draw back far enough, do you see how small you are in the grand scheme of things, but also how beautiful and *integral*? It is amazing that you are here, consciously thinking, *What is this?* It is magnificent that you are here, breathing, whatever it is that you are. Do you feel yourself dissolving in this awareness? Do you feel a little scared, as if you are only just now realizing how many things had to take place in order for you to be here, this exact moment…and how fleeting your time is, how small these problems seem in the face of all this **great mystery**?

What is there to hold on to? Is there even a "you" to hold on to? What then, is this little moment of pain? Isn't it precious, too? What then is this feeling of separation? An illusion.

"When the vessel and its contents are filled with negativities, transform these unfavorable conditions into the path to enlightenment"

It is very easy to be virtuous, generous, kind, loving, and a good friend when things are happy and everything is smooth sailing. I can afford to be benevolent and listen to your problems when things are going well for me—when, for instance, I have love and stability in my life. But the second things turn, my boyfriend leaves and I have a house payment to make on my own, business goes awry, my health suffers, I'm lonely and cranky—well then it's understandable that I'm not very nice and generous, right?

But of course, this is actually the best time to practice being something other than awful to other people. Life is *always* going to throw us curve balls. It is *always* going to rock the boat just when we are getting particularly settled. It is not an excuse to become a miserable wretch. Yes, I say this knowing that I have most certainly used it as an excuse to be a miserable wretch. It is very difficult not to take our pain out on others, or to be negligent because of what we're dealing with—which is usually a very good wallow in self-pity. But this is the best material for true practice—an exercise in transformation. Can we take the shit that is thrown our way and use it as fertilizer? Can we take the troubling things that happen and use them to grow and to help others to grow? Don't give in to the temptation to use grief as a shield or as a bludgeon where we strike out because we can't attack the thing that is hurting us directly. The pain that is in your heart right now? **Imagine that you can reach it by touching it in someone else with the intent to heal it.** We are all connected.

"Put all the blame on the one"

Most likely, you've been spending a lot of time blaming. (Guess what? I don't blame you.) It's hard because we want to hold someone responsible for all this suffering. We want to find someone at fault so that we can place the burden of our suffering at their feet. We want to say that they are wrong, and so they should say they are sorry. They should take responsibility for their actions.

Unfortunately, this blaming is doing no good whatsoever. What's more, if you are looking for someone to hold responsible for your suffering, I'm going to have to tell you something you will not like to hear.

YOU are the one responsible.

"Oh, unfair!" you might say. "I was the very picture of perfection, and he was an awful toad who did unspeakable things to me." Well look, he may have been an awful toad, but now he's an *absent* awful toad. That means that all the terrible things you think he's still doing to you are now falling squarely on you. All this anger, frustration, and the need you have for him to call you up at four in the morning, preferably sobbing and telling you how sorry he is for being so cruel (or the need you may have to call him up and tell him what a miserable son-of-a-bitch he is) is only torturing YOU.

No one wants to take the blame for anything—even when something is legitimately our fault. We want to come up with excuses... find some way to pass the buck. We can't stand to be wrong, but worse, *much* worse, we can't stand to take responsibility for something that most definitely does *not* feel like our fault. It's unfair, and we have a very sophisticated and overdeveloped sense for sniffing out injustice.

But if we're willing to stop and consider what the result of all this blaming is, and we're willing to take responsibility for our own actions, then we are suddenly on the fast-track to being able to wish honestly that others may be free from suffering. If we take the blame on ourselves, what a relief! What a weight off our shoulders! Now we can all get something accomplished because we're not caught up in arguing over who is at fault—and then waiting for that person to make it right. Think of all that energy you've been expending in feeling how unfair it all is...well, it's perfectly fair. Who should take responsibility for the state of YOU if not YOU?

Things did not work out between you and your ex, and who has a problem? Well, let's take my situation, for example. Clearly, since I was unhappy with the way James was treating me, this became *my* problem. He did not have a problem with the way he was treating me. He might have carried on for an eternity that way, going out all the time, coming in late and drunk, not working or bringing in a steady income, then yelling at me for daring to cook breakfast in the kitchen while he was also trying to cook breakfast. He was fine with it! I was the one with the problem. So, okay.

Maybe your ex hit you. You didn't like it, but I'm guessing he was okay with it because he was doing it. He might have said he was sorry after the fact, but then he went and did it again, so there wasn't a problem in his mind. He hit you, and felt bad for a second, and then hit you again. But YOU didn't like it. So, okay.

Let's say your ex left you suddenly. Out of the blue, he gets up one day and says he is leaving. He doesn't love you. Maybe he never loved you, and he's only now figuring it out. But all the while you adored him! How could this be your responsibility now? How can it be your responsibility now if your ex was mistaking you for a punching bag? Why can't you keep blaming him, because he has to be the one responsible, right? It should be, because he was awful. It should be his fault that he didn't love you enough to treat you nicely and care for you. Or maybe it's God's fault, because God let it happen. God did not sit him down and say, "Look buddy. I brought you a good woman, and now you must love her."

The flip-side of this is a lot of self-pity. "Okay," you may say. "If I can't blame him, then it must be all my fault because I'm such an awful person."

You might start making up stories of why this is your fault. Perhaps you gained a few pounds, or you shouldn't have asked him all those questions about the house while he was in a bad mood, or maybe you didn't like bacon pizza and beer, and he might have been nicer if you could have eaten Burger King with him or sat in the bar with him getting drunk and watching football, or maybe wrestling with him in your underwear, growling like grizzly bears.

But I'm not suggesting that you simply try to blame yourself for *his* actions. This is neurotic. Also, it's deceptive because deep down, we're really still blaming someone else for being so shallow as to have not overlooked our weight or dislike for bacon pizza—and so now it's *also* their fault for making us feel bad about ourselves! I mean, it's not our fault he's such an asshole.

Stop!

I know it's an incredibly radical thought, but this act of taking responsibility for *how you feel and act right now*—including this desire you have of blaming someone else and wanting retribution—is really just another way of taking in the suffering and pain of others and sending back out love, joy, and healing. It is about honoring our choices, and honoring their choices, too. We don't have to like them. Chances are, we didn't like them, and that's why we're in this situation.

I could say that you got yourself into this. Does that sound true? It may not have been what you pictured in your head. Someone took a turn down a road you didn't intend to go down, and sure enough, the road was full of Rodents of Unusual Size, maybe poison ivy...you have a hell of a rash now, and the fire and quicksand slowed you down. So you said to hell with this road! I'm getting out of here.

Good choice.

When I examine my own relationship through this lens, I see that I could have chosen not to have a problem with any of it. I could have been very laid-back and unconcerned with his behavior and its impact upon my own behavior. Things may have turned out differently, or they might have turned out the same. But that's all irrelevant because I *did* have a problem with it, and so it ended. I take full responsibility.

I could blame him for not loving me enough, but the truth is also that I didn't love ME enough all those times I let things happen that felt wrong for me and my life. And finally, I didn't love HIM enough to keep on letting things happen as they did. The truth is that in the end, I wanted to honor myself more than I wanted to honor him. So, okay. Here we are. We don't have to keep railing against the injustice of it all. It's all very just.

But maybe you didn't have any control over the ending of your relationship, so it feels different. Now what you are left with is how you are making yourself feel every single hour of the day. *That* is what you're responsible for now. That is what you must own.

"MEDITATE ON EVERYONE AS KIND"

Yes, that includes the person who just kindly broke your heart. The fact of the matter is, without such people in our lives, how would we grow? Every event that makes us unhappy is a chance to practice equanimity, grace, kindness, patience, tolerance—everything! These people hurting us are actually being quite kind by providing such opportunities! Yes, this sounds like sarcasm, but it's not. (Not really. Okay, a little bit.) Remember, "Thank you for everything, I have no complaint whatsoever"?

How can we learn to be grateful for these aggravations? I'll give you an example.

Right now, I live on a very noisy street. I have certain neighbors who are like Squidbillies (anthropomorphic hillbilly squids, named after the *Adult Swim* TV show, in case you were wondering). They go into the street late at night and yell profanities at each other. They are scary to look at, and at first, they were frightening to live near. When I think of this experience, and the fact that I'm in this house to begin with because of my relationship and the choices we made as a couple, it becomes difficult not to feel upset…resentful. It feels unfair. But then I remember that I made this choice, too. It was for a different life than I'd imagined, but here I am—and now all that's left is the reality of the situation. I have scary, noisy neighbors. This is what I have to work with. This is one of the sharp stones helping me to slough off old skin.

I like quiet when I want it to be quiet. I like it so much that it makes me very angry not to have it. So then I start yelling. I want my neighbors to stop yelling or bouncing a basketball at midnight, so I'm in my house yelling and pounding around adding to the general chaos of the situation. There's noise everywhere, and I have very little control over it. This is reality. I like quiet, and my neighbors are noisy. I may get mad, and there is part of me that's observing, a little amused. Yes, there's that feeling of wanting to throw a tantrum over a little noise. Okay, there's me *actually* throwing a tantrum over a little noise. Work with it.

But that's the easier stuff. Being grateful to my ex for breaking my heart is not as easy. Feeling as if his actions have been a kindness is laughable—except that what is possible on the other end of such things, things that are life-changing for us, *can* be downright miraculous.

Great pain can cause us to break down so many of the illusions that we've built up around ourselves. It makes us vulnerable. It can make us hyperaware of others and of ourselves—and this is golden. This is the treasure of surrendering to the fire. We're being melted down and life is shaping us, like steel, into some useful tool—if we let it. That means being strong enough to let the process work on us, to see it through to completion without immediately searching for whatever it is that will make us numb and forgetful—alcohol, pills, sex, rebound relationships, etc.

I am saying it's a hard journey, but the treasure you're seeking is you. A calmer you. A happier you. A you that doesn't rely on other people to assign your value or bring you a sense of love and joy.

Life is the best teacher, just as it is. It is the toughest teacher. It won't tolerate slothfulness for long. It's always throwing some difficult problem your way and then seeing what you will do with it. "What is the point of all this?" you might ask.

To wake up, and to stay awake for as long as possible.

Be grateful to everyone who can grab you by the shoulders and jolt you awake. This can bring you closer to yourself—something we should consider to be a great kindness.

"ALWAYS RELY ON MENTAL HAPPINESS ALONE"

I am mentioning this as a possibility. I know how hard it is. We're constantly trying to think of reasons why we *should* be happy, considering something awful just happened to us. What is there to be joyful about?

You. Let's start there. You have an opportunity to make big changes. Not only are you no longer tied down, but also, you are free to be REAL about yourself. Let's face it—when we're in a relationship, there's always a little bit of us that seems subjugated, merged with the other person—and then there's the perpetual dance of trying to be pleasing and agreeable and accommodating, which doesn't always work. Then there's our emotional state, anger, manipulation, trying to get this other person to do what we want or to accept what we want to do for ourselves—but now we are on our own. We're shaken to the very core. Vulnerable. In pain. We now have a chance to embrace all this shaking. So many opportunities! Is it possible to allow yourself to feel some small measure of peace over this? A popular quote (author unknown) asks, *"What if you woke up today with only the things you thanked God for yesterday?"* What would that be for you?

"Do not hold a grudge"

Sometimes, it's hard to go against our normal nature. We have been struck—we've taken a sledgehammer to the heart. It's a knee-jerk reaction to want to kick something. But then the knee-jerk reaction hangs on. We want to kick something *all the time*. We start wanting to kick other people, ourselves—everything is fair game.

Life has just thrown you for a loop, encouraging you to break free from old patterns and ways of being. So why be predictable in your responses and in your actions?

After the breakup, James and I discussed the house. He assumed I would leave to move back to be near family, especially because I had a very portable job and no friends or firm ties to the community. He knew how much I disliked the neighborhood.

I told him, "No. I will learn to live here." Of course, when I said it, I was being defiant. "Take THAT, you HEARTBREAKER." I wanted to prove to him how tough I was. But this small rebellion served me. When I say not to be predictable in your approach, I also mean, don't take the easy way. Anger is the easy way. Giving up is the easy way. The easy way may be giving in to a knee-jerk emotional reaction. "You jerk! I'll show *you*. I'll do something stupid that doesn't benefit me at all!" It's also drowning yourself in temporary comforts, curling up with your chosen mithridates and settling in to numbness.

It would have been much easier for me to move away—to run away from the house and the city so that I could be taken care of, but there was also a fire in me to make changes in my life, to make friends, to be part of a community that inspired me. I knew what awaited me if I moved but not what awaited me if I stayed.

Don't be predictable, and don't hold on to feelings that lead you down the easy, safer path. The most beneficial path? It might be the one you are afraid to walk.

"Train in what is most difficult"

Since we are working to utilize this horrific experience as an opportunity for self-improvement, there are a few things we must try very hard to do.

1. We must recognize when we are behaving in a way that is crazy!

We might call this being neurotic, or driving ourselves and others nuts; however you want to put it. Crazy is crazy.

This is hard to do—mainly because we always want to think of ourselves as the good guy. It's everyone *else* who has the problem, not us. Everyone else is annoying and selfish. We're just trying to help them by pointing it out.

I once knew someone who abhorred self-examination and self-justification. When someone asked him to question or examine his own behavior, he would become absolutely livid. How dare they! He would go on to distract you by pointing out your own less-than-perfect behavior and encourage you to examine it closely instead. He kept close watch on how everyone else acted but absolutely could not turn that light on himself.

This is understandable. It's frightening to do so. "Our loathing of dirt may be so great as to prevent our cleaning ourselves—'justifying' ourselves" (Nietzsche). When we are really asked to look at our behavior, it's usually the last thing we'd like to do. When others point out things that are less than flattering, our egos normally get involved. We become defensive. We may lash out and try to take the attention away from ourselves—try to infect other people with our zombie brain-munchers—but if we are very serious about growing, about becoming a better person, this has to stop. It's very hard, but step one is to recognize when we are being unreasonable, crazy, neurotic jerks. At first, seeing it may be all that we can do.

"Oh," you might say, while you're in the middle of yelling at your mother for not telling you what you want to hear, "there I am being angry and mean and selfish." Even while you're saying this in your head, you're still being angry and mean and selfish. You're still thinking that she should change to accommodate YOU—which is typically what we think the entire world should do.

So, in the beginning, all you can do is recognize it while it's happening. Eventually, when you practice seeing your actions long enough, you will come to a point where you can actually stop yourself. You may feel all that angry, mean energy swelling up within you, your eyes get all squinty and your heart speeds up, you're almost ready to breathe fire in someone's face, but then you stop. You take a breath. You unfasten yourself from the surface-to-air missile.

Even further down the road, you may be able to keep from getting worked up in the first place. It's not just that you recognize, or recognize and stop before you act out your feelings but that they are superseded altogether by feelings of compassion or love or acceptance.

I tell you this: if you hate self-examination, you should train to self-examine in *everything*. Then hold yourself accountable for absolutely *everything*. There is no one who knows you like you do. You know when you are trying to fool others. You know when you are trying to trick yourself. Look, you're not doing yourself any favors, and you're not helping anyone else either. Asking everyone else to be accountable while refusing to be accountable is not only a double standard but it's also completely counterproductive to any kind of personal growth.

Where you are in your life right now is the result of a series of steps you have taken, choices you have made. You are responsible. Don't blame you mother and father. Don't blame your brother or sister. Don't blame your son or daughter. Don't blame your ex-partner. Don't blame your teachers. Don't blame society, or the president, or your congressman. Don't blame your boss. Don't blame God. Don't complain that Santa Claus didn't bring you the toy that you wanted, and it's not fair. Everyone else is getting along so much better in the world, and you have always gotten a raw deal. Listen, I'm like you! I think it's unfair, too. Life is handing out lemons to me while everyone else is getting Bentleys. So I can commiserate. But deep down, I know it's not true. There are people in the world who are starving and living in dirt hovels drinking tainted water—all with more grace and equanimity than I have waking up in my house with all my toys and gadgets surrounding me—only I'm sad because my heart is broken, or because I think I'm not living the life I should be living because other people have done one thing or another to make it hard. There are people dying who are braver, stronger, and more cheerful than I am on my best day. What is our excuse then? How do we justify continuing to be awful to everyone? Why do we keep on thinking we always know what is best for others? How can we stop living our lives from a place of fear?

2. Stop expecting it to all make sense.

We are searching for meaning in what happened. We're trying to find some way to make it all make sense. We want it to make sense because we think that if only we're able to make sense of it all, it won't hurt so much. We'll be able to accept what happened and move on because we'll know *why* it happened. It's the senselessness of it that kills us. We can't imagine a God—at least not a loving God—who would allow us to hurt this much. How could he give us this heart, this capacity to love, and present us with someone *to* love, and then rip it all away so brutally? How do we make it make sense?

It doesn't *need* to make sense. That's also to say that you can ascribe whatever meaning to it that you need to. That's usually what we spend most of our time doing with *everything*—classifying, categorizing, defining. But consider why we're trying to make sense of it all anyway. We just want to be told it will all be okay in the end. We'll get what we want. This relationship didn't work out because Prince Charming is waiting around the corner up ahead and we needed to learn these lessons first. While this might be true, it might not be true. If you can't accept that, and you absolutely need something to hold onto, then try this:

The person waiting for you around the corner, the person dying to know you, adore you, love you

is You.

And while that might not feel completely satisfactory right this moment, it's one thing that makes perfect sense. It's the one thing we can absolutely know to be true.

3. Don't be afraid of love.

You may be feeling a real sense of fear now that you are on your own. This fear may be born of a sense of division. You have suffered a great loss, and it automatically feels as if you've been disconnected from *all* things—even yourself, perhaps even your understanding of a higher power or universal energy. This leaves you floundering in the unknown. Worse, it feels like you've been disconnected from your own heart. What is love to this new, very raw person? What good does love do if it causes this much pain? Love is bullshit, you decide. It doesn't exist. It's just a word. End of story.

Look. What's bullshit is the way people use that word to tie others to a cart load of expectations. Love's only task is to undo ME. It's not a performance. It's not a "get out of suffering free" card. Love is not to blame; it's our ideas on what that love should be doing that are to blame.

Love doesn't owe me anything, and loving someone doesn't mean that person owes me anything either—including any kind of return on my emotional investment. Here's what I get: I *see* them, their divine beauty, and that seeing goes all the way down into myself.

Remember, love—life in general—is a very useful tool for creation. Love doesn't want your chocolates and flowers and empty promises of forever. Love/Life wants the *product* of love. It is, after all, perhaps one of the most powerful tools we have to create, reveal, and transform.

However, the manner of that transformation is something I cannot dictate. I cannot make someone else feel my love—let alone force them to return it. All I can ask is this: "Does some energy of *mine* keep transforming *me* in a way that feels useful?" Great! If some energy of *yours* also happens to transform *you* in a way that feels useful, great! If not, what are we doing?

This kind of freedom allows my presence in any relationship to be a choice, not a contractual obligation. Trading on love immediately removes me from it. When I trade on love (I'll give you affection if you do what I want), it costs me the freedom to be authentic.

Together, we have the chance to create something powerful. That could mean children, or it could mean creating something powerful within ourselves that then goes on and impacts others. I still hold firm to the belief that the best partners *amplify* each other. They do not *possess* each other. They do not *damage* each other. They do not seek to *change* each other into little dancing puppets.

So, ask yourself this: Was your last partnership creating things or tearing them down? Were you wrapped up in your relationship to the exclusion of all else? Is what you are creating right now superior to what you were creating then? Do you at least see the potential for creation, for transformation?

Keep working. Be honest. Be compassionate. Take care of yourself. Take care of others. We are all suffering. May we all be free. May we help to free others.

"THERE IS A storm coming."

These were the words of my mother, who always seems to know about the weather before I do. She lives two hours away, but it's not unusual for her to be alert to weather events I wouldn't have noticed until my house blew down.

This news did nothing to improve my mood. I had been feeling very low that day. This was directly related to a resurgence of dreams about James, and in all of them, I found myself trying to get back together with him. Also in all of them, he kept rejecting me. It made for slightly less-than-pleasant mornings, and the dreams hovered over me like dark clouds.

"Is it supposed to be bad?" I asked.

"Yes."

"All right," I said, sighing. I knew what that meant: a little bit of Friday night spent in my spider-infested, mold-coated basement.

I turned on the TV and tuned to the weather. Sure enough, it looked to be a bad one. They were calling for 80 mph winds, which is highly unusual for the Mid-Ohio valley. There would be lightning and hail—maybe a little fire and brimstone, if you wanted to believe The Weather Channel's take on things.

I kept the volume up high as I began going through the house collecting the items I would want with me should my house get sucked up in a tornado and then relocated to Oz: computer back-up drives, a thumb drive containing personal writing projects, my purse, keys, cell phone, tablet, laptop… Getting the dog into the basement was easy. Getting the cat, who always seemed to sense when I really needed for him to do something (providing him with a fun opportunity to do the opposite) required an ambush. Finally, I was prepared to—as Floridians say—"hunker down."

The storm came in fast. The sky grew dark, and the lights began to flicker. My mom, who was still holding on the line, asked me where I was.

"I'm in the basement, but I keep losing power," I told her. The air conditioner unit was kicking on and then off again as the lights did the same. I dug out a battery-operated lantern from my old Florida hurricane kit and turned it on. I could see the trees buffeting back and forth violently through the small basement windows. I could also see Roy and his son sitting out on their back porch. Not much scares them enough to go inside…apparently, not even 80 mph winds. Debris was falling all around, but I was primarily focused on the flickering power and the on again, off again of the A/C.

Worried that the surges might cause damage to the unit, I said, "I'm going to go up and turn it off."

"Don't go upstairs!" she told me.

"Too late," I said. "I'm already up here." It was still very dark out, and the winds were really ferocious. Quickly, I flicked the thermostat from Cool to the Off position and went to peer out the window.

That's when I smelled it.

"That's odd," I said.

"What?" my mother asked.

"I smell smoke."

Immediately, I began walking around my house, sniffing at the air. Storm be damned. Wind doesn't scare me nearly as much as a Burning Building. I could survive a little huffing and puffing just fine in my basement (assuming the house didn't fall down, of course). But a little crackle and blaze and various sizzling of combustibles…not so much.

The smell didn't seem to be upstairs, but when I returned to the window downstairs, I smelled it again. The window had a ridiculously poor seal, so I thought it might be coming from something outside. Surely no one was *barbecuing* in the storm, I thought—although I wouldn't necessarily put it past the drunken college boys who were liberally dotted along my street (like a neighborhood case of pox).

The wind was dying down a bit, and I deemed it safe enough to venture out onto my back porch.

The smell was immediately stronger.

I surveyed the yard. Roy and his son were now out in their back driveway, looking up.

"Whoa!" Roy said, then he laughed.

What's so funny? I wondered.

My head lifted, my eyes seeking....

Oh. There.

"Fire."

"What?" she asked.

"There's a fire out here," I told my mother. "I'll call you back."

At the rear of their yard, you could see flames high up in a tree that straddled their property. Smoke was beginning to billow. The smell was getting stronger...and surprisingly, the rain was *not* putting it out.

"Did you call the fire department?" I called out. I could hear sirens in the distance, so I thought they might have already phoned it in.

"No," Roy said.

Why the hell not? I wanted to shout. When you see fire, is the best time to call the fire department after you know for *certain* that it's going to catch your house on fire—because your house is actually on fire—or *before*, sort of like a preventative method?

I grabbed for my phone and dialed 911 myself.

And...it was busy.

A busy signal at 911. The hairs on the back of my neck stood up.

No one was coming. At least not right that moment, and the fire didn't appear to be going out. It didn't take much imagination to see the potential for it to ignite stuff I totally dig not having ignited.

I went back inside. This time, I reversed the process of storm preparation. I grabbed everything I'd previously toted downstairs, including the dog and cat, and began loading them into my car. Once that was done, I began adding to it. *Question:* If there were only one inanimate object you could carry with you in the event of a fire, what would it be? *Answer:* My computer. I might even walk into a burning building for it. Maybe. I mean, if there were a way I could biologically bond with my computer, become some sort of hybrid Intel-branded cyborg, then by God, a double eyelash blink would serve as the default "post picture to Facebook" and the entirety of my friend's list would already be sharing in this snapshot of me hyperventilating.

But still finding myself to be disappointingly organic, I had to pause on one of my trips in from the car to put my head between my legs and breathe. Passing out on the kitchen floor would most likely count as an epic fail in the category of "things to do in the event of an emergency."

When I went back outside, I saw that there was ash falling, drifting over to me on the wind. The bottom of my skirt was dragging in the mud. I was now wet, dotted with ash, hyperventilating, and tripping on a muddy skirt—all perfectly exciting stuff that I could do without.

Once I had the car loaded with essentials, I moved on to the task of alerting my *other* neighbor—the one not dancing around beneath the falling embers.

I knocked on Brad and his wife Tracy's back door for what felt like an eternity. I was prepared to give up, assuming they weren't home, when finally Brad opened the door and poked his head around the screen.

"Hey there," I said. "Just a friendly head's up. There's a tree on fire over there."

"Wow!" he said, smiling. "That's something to know."

Brad is infinitely cool. He never gets stressed about anything. His lack of stress immediately causes you to dial down your own. You can't help it. Stress absolutely cowers in the face of his good-natured calm.

I found myself smiling back at him as he bent his head to see underneath the awning and over the privacy fence that blocks off his patio from our shared driveway.

"What are those guys doing over there?" he asked, referring to Roy and his son.

"Cheering on the fire, I presume." Indeed, they were now hooting at the fire in addition to the occasional "Whoa!" as large embers tumbled onto their garage. Yes. Little bits of flamey things, falling from the sky and burning stuff.

I suddenly chuckled. I had reached critical mass. Everything was now entirely ridiculous.

"I tried calling 911," I told him, "but it was busy. A recording told me that it was storing my number for a callback. It's official," I added. "I consider this to be the apocalypse."

Brad laughed. "Those guys aren't going to let the neighborhood burn down," he said, nodding his head in their general direction.

I shrugged, dubious. "I'm not so sure," I said. "I'm waiting for them to break out the hot dogs and marshmallows."

"Well, I have beer." Brad was still smiling. "Anyway, it's going to be okay."

"Can you say that again?" I asked. It had been a long time since I'd heard a man say it. I sorely needed to hear it in that moment.

"It's going to be okay." He laughed again. "Do you need a hug?"

I contemplated this person with whom I'd communicated over fence lines for nearly twelve months, sharing cookies and random chitchat. He'd pet my dog in the mornings on his way to work, or drag my trashcan back up from the curb.

"Yes," I finally said. "I do."

He came over to me and grabbed me up. It wasn't an "I don't know you, so I'm going to barely touch you" kind of hug. It was a bear hug.

"Thank you," I said, meaning it deeply.

And what do you know? While all of this was going on, the fire was finally beginning to respond to the rain. Its flickers were becoming frail. It was licking at the trunk of the tree with a great deal less enthusiasm. I felt confident then that the rain would put it out. Our houses were safe. Good thing, too.

The firemen never did come. It turns out they had plenty to keep them busy.

The aftermath was tremendous. The storm itself lasted only twenty-five minutes, but in its wake it left 345,000 people in our region without power. It left trees uprooted and lying across roads or houses. Power lines fell, trapping people in their cars. Fires broke out. Half the city was suddenly dark.

But, miracle of miracles…I had power. I was one of the lucky ones. Power meant Air Conditioning, and this was critical given the fact that we were *also* being hit with a very uncharacteristic heat wave. Temperatures had been in the upper nineties, and we were forecast to get higher…the following week was going to turn triple-digit.

When things calmed down, I decided to make a quick trip to the grocery store (where I planned to buy something as a thank you to Brad for being so cool). Once I made it off my own street, I realized the destruction that had taken place around me. All the street lights were out. So were the traffic lights. A large tree blocked half the road down which I was traveling. By the time I reached the grocery store, I saw that it still had power, but it also held a mass of people who had come out to get batteries and ice. Lines in every lane extended down nearly every aisle of the store.

I turned back around and left. I couldn't think of a single thing I needed badly enough to stand in that line.

Again, I was one of the lucky ones.

Power restoration was slow. The next day, lines of vehicles strayed out into the roadway as people waited at the few gas stations that still had power. People were filling their tanks and gas cans to fuel their generators. In fact, there were no more generators to be had in the Lowe's that still had lights, and no more batteries. They sold out of everything that first night. Unlike a hurricane in a region such as Florida, where you have days to prepare, this storm came from nowhere, and no one had been ready.

I finally gave up trying to get gas during the day. I waited until midnight to fill up, and I still had to drive out of my neighborhood to find a station that had gas as well as power. My area had been one of the hardest hit.

I spent the weekend updating on Facebook, offering any of those without power the option of coming to my house to cool down, to charge up their phones, whatever was needed. I felt blessed and wanted to pass it on.

Lucky. Lucky Me.

It was on the third day that my luck began to wane.

On my way back home from running errands, I noticed a fire truck parked in front of the house that shared a back fence with me. *A little late,* I thought, in a feeble attempt to make light of the situation. *I called three days ago!*

But I wasn't laughing. I had a feeling that this fire truck was a harbinger of unpleasant things to come.

When I pulled in to my parking space, I saw firemen looking up at the power line on the other side of the fence, but I didn't see anything wrong. Eventually they went away, so I went inside, put my keys on the counter, and realized that I could hear the back-up battery on the power supply for my computer beeping. A quick check of the house revealed that some of the power appeared to be off, including the part that powered the A/C.

I didn't immediately make the connection. Instead, I went down to the fuse box, assuming something had blown. None of the fuses were off. I flipped them anyway. Nothing. I went upstairs and outside, where I could always be sure to get a neighborhood update from Roy.

"Do you have power?" I shouted over the fence.

"In half the house," he said.

"How odd! Me, too." *How weird can you get?* I thought. Power in only *half* the house? Clearly it wasn't an issue with the fuse if my neighbor was having the same trouble.

That's when Brad's wife, Tracy, appeared.

"I called the fire department before," she told me. "The wires out here were sparking while you were gone. They came out but said there wasn't anything they could do. It had stopped by then."

"And now there's no power," I said.

She shrugged. "I have power in half the house."

Wow. All three of us. Half of our houses.

"It's because we're on two lines," Roy called out, directing my attention to the lines running above my head.

I looked up. Sure enough, there were two power lines trailing to the house. So one of them was up, and one of them was down. Who ever heard of such a thing? Certainly not my landlord, who was my next call.

"Are you sure?" he asked. "Did you go check the fuse box?"

I sighed. *I'm really pretty smart,* I wanted to tell him. Instead, I said, "Yes. It's not the fuse box—especially considering the fact that it's happening to my neighbors as well."

Naturally, there was nothing he could do, and I had a feeling we might be dealing with this half-power situation for a while, since half of the city was still without power altogether. We weren't going to be high on their list of priorities—although I *did* have to wonder, given that the lines had been sparking, whether this constituted a "dangerous power situation." When I called the electric company to add my outage to the thousands of reports they already had on file, the woman told me that they wouldn't consider it dangerous.

"Really?" I asked. *Lines shooting out sparks pretty okay in your book, then?* What did I know? High voltage was fairly far outside my realm of expertise.

Regardless, I decided to count my blessings that I still had HALF power.

Lucky me.

The temperature was climbing, and it was already growing incredibly warm in the house. The sun was streaming in, and the thermostat climbed two degrees while I stood there, contemplating the next step.

Thankfully, I had a window A/C unit stored in the basement. The only problem was that there was no way I could install it by myself. It was too heavy for me to carry and secure on my own. I'd been considering finding a general handyman for things I couldn't handle, and prior to this event, I'd settled on the man my landlord used for house repairs. I had his business card in my kitchen drawer. Immediately, I called him, praying he was available. I was already sweating. The temperature outside was 98 degrees. The temperature inside was 82—up from 78 just thirty minutes before.

"I'm so glad you're there," I said, when John picked up the phone. I told him who it was and then launched into my desperate plea. I explained the situation and then added, "There's no power to the A/C, and I can't get my window unit in by myself. Can you help?"

He told me he would be glad to help, and that he would be sending his son-in-law. At that point, he could have sent a koala wearing floppy shoes and an ascot, as long as he could install the damn thing before the temperature got any higher.

While I waited for the handyman's stand-in to arrive, I began redirecting power. I found my heavy load extension cords and set about re-routing power to my microwave, what would be the window unit, computer, modem, router, and television. The refrigerator was still operational, and I was very glad for it. But, of course, cool air was also fairly high on my list of priorities. A quick glimpse again at the thermostat showed

85 degrees.

Sweat beaded my forehead. I stopped to get a drink.

When I turned on the faucet, the most horrendous odor of *gasoline* emerged.

"Moses, Mary, and Vishnu, what *the fuck*?!" I shouted.

I went outside again. Back to check the neighborhood news.

"Roy, does your water smell funny?"

He nodded. "Yeah, it's smelled funny for days now," he said. "Somebody hit a gas line when they were working on the power."

I frowned, failing to understand what someone hitting a gas line days ago would have to do with my water smelling like *gasoline*. Certainly my water hadn't smelled like this for *days* either. It didn't make sense, but then again, I could tell that he was beginning to place me in the category of "foolish womenfolk." Men (especially of the very manly sort) can be terribly pragmatic at times. Life is simple: Tarzan hunt game. Jane cook meat (when she's not too busy acting hysterical).

"Just run it for a while; it'll be fine," he said, laughing at the look on my face (a look like I'd just smelled something foul—gasoline mixed with my water, for example).

I must have *also* looked dubious because he added, "I thought you were a country girl?"

I shook my head. "My mother's side is from West Virginia, but I grew up here," I told him.

"Same difference, right?" he asked.

Not even close, I thought. Unless by "country girl" he meant girl who is practically having a love affair with technology. I knit afghans using Cat 5 cable and milk gigabytes from the teats of USB flash drives. I mean, we had power when I was growing up, for goodness'

sake. We're not Amish. Or cavemen. If anything, I was lamenting not having solar panels or a generator. I love nature as much as the next person, but I'm the sort of camper who delights in…well, a *camper*. You know, the kind with a toilet, electricity, satellite dish, wifi…

But I digress. We were talking about the water. I can tell you one thing: there was no way that I was just going to *run the water*, which smelled like I was fueling up at the Shell station whenever I turned the tap, and then DRINK it. Was he kidding?!

More stress! The thing I do when I'm stressed is generally fix myself a cup of Ginger tea. (Which is my cure-all for every ailment known to man, by the way.) But I couldn't do that. Why? Because THERE WASN'T ANY DRINKABLE WATER! There was nothing to drink in the house at all, in fact. I'm a tea or water drinker. That's what I drink. Tea. Or water. Dammit.

While I was considering all of this, there was a knock at my door.

The boy on the other side of the screen didn't look any older than twenty-one. He was covered in tattoos and had on a sweat-soaked muscle shirt. He was also cute, and I was mindful of the fact that I looked like I'd just been set into a pot of boiling water (which, incidentally, smelled like gasoline).

I patted at my hair, tugged down my shirt, and directed him to the window A/C unit, which he easily lifted and carried up from the basement. He did a great job of installing it and sealing it off. It took about ten minutes. When he was done, I asked how much I owed him, thinking $25 to $50 ought to cover it.

"That will be $75," he told me.

I blinked. *Wow. That's a lot of money for your muscle—and you didn't even take off your shirt,* I thought, writing out the check, feeling like a victim of highway robbery and a dirty old woman at the same time. I was also thinking, *Note to self: Acquire more manly men friends!*

The A/C unit worked fine. I went to the store to get bottled water and then settled down, gratefully sipping my tea.

I could breathe a little easier (so long as I didn't turn on the faucet). I could use the microwave and toaster oven. My food wasn't spoiling. I could even watch a movie.

Lucky.

Regardless, I didn't sleep well that night. I'd turned off the A/C when I went to bed, afraid to run it too much, believing I might run it down. Go ahead and laugh. What did I know? The only thing I knew was that the A/C seemed like a precious commodity that was possibly finite. If I could have wrapped the unit in swaddling clothes and sung it a lullaby, I would have. But my overprotectiveness meant that by 8AM, when it was already in the eighties outside and HUMID, the house was sticky-warm.

Immediately I turned the air back on. But the temperature outside was so hot, so early, that no part of the house cooled down to any reasonable degree but the dining room, which was the only room that could accommodate the window unit. I spent the morning moving everything to within a foot of the A/C…a recliner, my laptop…then I spent the afternoon in front of the blower, trying to stay cool as the temperature outside climbed to an obscene 102 degrees. The only bathroom in my house was upstairs, and I had to give myself a little psychological pep talk in order to use it. It was easily over 110 degrees in there, and stifling. I plugged a fan into the bathroom outlet (part of the house that still worked) and set it to blow air at me while I was brushing my teeth (with bottled water).

The dog, cat, and I had become dining room camp refugees. There wasn't much to do but sit in the recliner, try to work on my laptop, and watch the thermostat continue to climb.

When it reached 88 degrees, I stopped looking.

Even once the sun set, the temperature didn't drop. At midnight, it was still 100 degrees. It was an uncomfortable night.

By morning, the dining room had cooled down to a positively frigid 79. It felt chilly enough compared to the previous dining room temperature of 88 that I put on a heavier shirt. Then I set about preparing for the day. I knew the temperature was supposed to reach 105, and my goal was to preserve as much of the current cool air in the house as possible. I would do this by blocking off all the windows, keeping out every ounce of sunlight.

As I wandered around the house gathering tools to make this happen, it occurred to me that I was doing this all on my own. By. My.

Self. I was "rolling with things" the best I could. I thought of James. Of course I did. I wondered whether he was somewhere in this town dealing with the very same situation or if he'd already moved on. If he was still staying with his mother, there was a good chance that they didn't have power. I hoped they were okay. I hoped he was taking good care of her. At the same time, I couldn't help but wonder what this situation would have been like had I not been alone. How would it be different if I had someone helping me through it? Certainly I wouldn't have had to pay someone $75 to install a window A/C!

On the other hand, I was doing just fine so far. That's what I told myself as I gathered as many blankets as I could find to cover the windows. The next question would be how to get them to stay in place. After dismissing the ideas of clothes-pinning them to the already existing curtains and duct-taping them (clearly ridiculous notions when considering the rules of gravity), I realized that I was going to have to nail them up.

Stepstool, hammer, nails—check.

I went about the house covering every window, and when I was done, the house was dark, cave-like. I prepared to spend another day in the dining room. After breakfast, I planned to get on my laptop and try to get more work done than I'd accomplished the day before. I had a lot of projects on my plate, and I was falling behind. Not being able to work out of my office was slowing me down *a lot*.

I was settling in to do just that when I happened to pull aside the heavy curtain in the kitchen to see outside.

There. In my back yard. Like spotting Santa Claus on Christmas Eve or a leprechaun with a pot of gold: two AEP power men staring up at the power lines.

I opened the door and stepped out onto my back porch, all smiles. I would have bowed down and kissed their feet. That is, until I found out what was actually going on.

"You got power?" one of the men asked.

I nodded. "Partial power," I said. "Two lines run to our houses, and one of them is out. No A/C," I added, hoping he would realize, you know, the absolute *gravity* of that last bit.

He nodded and adjusted his hard hat. "Well…we're gonna have to shut 'er down," he said.

"Oh great—err…I mean, *what?!*" I said. "Uh, to get it back on-line, right?" I asked, hopeful.

He shrugged. "That's for the boss to decide. But we gotta do it. That line is dangerous, and I can't leave it up."

Oh, so *now* they decide it's dangerous. Before, when it was, you know, *shooting off sparks* it was fine.

The man walked off, presumably to talk to his boss, and I was left standing there—the reality of the situation slowly sinking in.

Neighbors emerged, a row of porches suddenly dotted with inquisitive heads popping up over fences. Evidently, the houses on the other side of Roy didn't have the benefit of two lines. They'd been without power for three days. We owed the miracle of AEP's appearance in our back yards to the neighbor down the way who literally stopped a power truck going down the street by stepping out in front of it. "It was either run me over or stop the truck. And then I kidnapped one of them," he told us all later. "That's the way you've got to do it."

I went into the house (careful to open and close the door as quickly as possible to keep in the cool air). Now I was infinitely grateful for having run the A/C all night and also for the morning's work of covering all the windows. That would, at least, buy me a little time while I figured out what to do. Braving 105-degree temperatures with no A/C seemed like a daunting task—like climbing Mount Everest if Mount Everest were in an Everest-sized oven.

Being proactive seemed to be the best thing to start with. First, I would run out and get ice. The food would keep in the freezer for a little while, at least. But I wanted to have some bags of ice on hand. There was a cooler in the basement. I also bought batteries.

Next, I dug up all my lanterns. With all the windows covered, it was dark in the house. I had plenty of flashlights, and plenty of battery-operated candles. But I wasn't really worried about the dark. That's because it seemed like the most reasonable final step would be to locate a hotel room that accepted pets. I wasn't sure yet that I would have to use it, but if the power wasn't restored some time that day, I knew that I might be forced to flee. By the time all of the cool air left the house, I would have to go, too. Luckily, I found that I could reserve a room, but I wouldn't be billed until I confirmed and checked in. I had until 6PM to make a decision, which left me seven hours to see how this played out.

Last but certainly not least, I located my battery-operated fan. This was a purchase I'd made years ago when I lived in Florida. It was part of the hurricane kit I'd put together. I'd never had a chance to use it. In fact, it was still unopened in its box. I took the time now to unwrap it.

It was a thing of beauty. A full twelve inches, this thing was *not* one of those personal fans that runs on AA batteries and is lucky to lift a strand of your hair if you hold it right in front of your face. Church fans made of old Sears catalog pages and Popsicle sticks generate more air flow. No, this baby ran on eight—count 'em—*eight* D batteries. I put in the ones I'd just bought at the store, turned it on, and was immediately blasted with a reasonably powerful surge of air. It might not have been blowing *cool* air, but psychologically, air MOVEMENT can do wonders for the morale.

Now that I was out of tasks, I decided to return to the porch to see what was going on.

The power men were back. They had a man with them who wasn't wearing a hard hat. I presumed he was the boss. I wanted to talk to him. I figured I could pump him for information under the guise of finding out whether I would need to move my car.

"Hi there!" I said brightly.

"Hi." He had a nice country accent. Pleasant.

"So, any word on whether you'll be able to work on us today?"

He nodded. "That's what we're aiming for," he said. "We have to trim trees first, and then we'll start."

"How long do you think it will take?" I asked.

"Hard to say," he said. "Could be sometime late tonight."

I was surprised. I kind of just assumed that all they had to do was climb a ladder, flip a few switches, and *presto!* Let there be light! Evidently, that was not the case.

Regardless, I smiled at him. I have to tell you, I put all the charm I could muster into that smile. There might even have been an eyelash flutter or two.

"We are SO grateful to you," I said. "It's awfully scary with no A/C in these temperatures." *Oh, please, Mr. Power Man, rescue me from that ol' rascally hot sun!* Eyelash flutter-flutter-flutter. If I'd been wearing a hoop-skirted dress with a low décolletage, I would have bent over and dangled it in front of him. (Also, if I'd had boobs enough to dangle.) Alas, I had no boob view to proffer in bribe. Just a smile and a breathy, "We appreciate whatever you can do."

He had me move my car, which I parked in back of Roy's house. Then it was just a matter of waiting.

Watching.

Waiting.

And trying to stay cool.

By noon, the temperature in the house was up again. I sat in front of my fan, spritzing water on myself and letting the fan blow me dry. I also spritzed water on the dog, who was mightily offended by this gesture of goodwill. *What the hell, lady?* he seemed to say, eyeing me with displeasure. He went to lie down beneath the kitchen table, presumably away from any more benevolent misting.

Every thirty minutes or so, I would creep out onto the back porch and observe the progress. First, it was HOT. HOT! As in, the only time I have ever experienced hotter temperatures was when I was traveling from California to Florida in July. While passing through Arizona it was so hot that I stopped at a hotel with air conditioning for *the day* so that I could start up again at night, when it felt like I'd be less likely to die were something to happen to the U-Haul in the middle of the desert. I'd made the mistake of leaving the plants in the car, and by evening, every single one of them was *burnt to a crisp.*

This kind of HOT felt like you were sitting in a pot of boiling water trying to breathe through a wet athletic sock tied around your mouth. I had stripped down to the thinnest spaghetti strap shirt and cotton skirt I owned. I sat on my porch, taking it in as best as I could. I was considering history, in fact.

In the old days, people didn't have air conditioning. Somehow, they didn't die. Of course, they also didn't have global warming, and the propensity to cut down every single tree within a five-mile radius of their house.

Plus, they weren't total sissies.

The bucket truck was finally trying to pull into my back yard. This, in and of itself, was a feat. The space between my house and

Brad's is essentially just wide enough to admit a car. If you weren't paying attention pulling into the driveway, you were going to scrape a house. (I know this from experience.) Of course, this was a giant bucket truck. It took an enormous amount of orchestration, guidance, lifting of power lines to accommodate the height of the truck; it took a man climbing on top of the truck to get past it, folding the side-view mirrors flat, and…uh…some minor scraping of houses to get that glorious hunk of machinery back there.

But they managed it, and the sight of them in my backyard was a thing of beauty. Every man out there—in their suspenders and hard hats, climbing into the bucket and rising up into the air—was gorgeous.

The rest was just waiting it out. I would sit on the porch for a while…acknowledging the wonder of their movements and also acknowledging the wonder of the fact that I was sitting out on my back porch on the hottest day of the year. Possibly the hottest day I'd ever experienced living in the Midwest. And I was MANAGING THE SITUATION. Meaning, I wasn't running away from it. I wasn't expecting someone else to come and rescue me (I mean, not counting the power guys). I wasn't freaking out. I wasn't cursing God. I was dealing with what was happening to the best of my abilities.

When it got too hot, I would slip back inside, into my dark cave of a house. I would sit on the floor in front of my battery fan, spritz more water, and text back and forth with friends. This helped to keep my mind off the rising temperature in the house. I was grateful.

And then, miracle of miracles, by 7:30 that evening,
POWER!

Oh, just the sound of the house coming back to life—the deep thrumming that announced the return of the refrigerator, the buzz of outlets, the rumble of juicy readiness—was electrifying! My house was waking up, waiting for me to insert items into its various outlets and GET SOMETHING DONE!

It was the best feeling. I felt drunk with joy.

The neighborhood spilled out onto back porches, and to the left and right of me, we all danced, we all laughed, we all cheered, and finally, we applauded the men who had brought us back cool air and cold beverages, microwaves and toaster ovens, televisions and computers. God bless us, every one.

That night, basking in the luscious luxury that is air conditioning, wallowing beneath a blaze of electric lights, soaking in the sounds of TV, surfing the seas of the Internet—a veritable ORGY of power—I felt a sense of peace. Standing in the shower (where the water no longer smelled of gasoline), I could literally feel the tension washing down and away from my body. Deep breath. It was the greatest release I'd known in quite some time. Life could return to normal. Sure, I would forget what this experience had been like. I would forget to fully appreciate having power, something we all take for granted. I would forget how Mother Nature can always wallop us. Drench us. Electrocute us. Drown us. Fry us. Wisk us away in tornadoes. But in that moment, something changed for me—something about my discomfort with this house, with my new station in it.

Getting back to normal meant the *new* normal. All along, I'd been fighting this house. Before this happened, I'd been considering finding another place to live—some place with fewer problems, crazy neighbors, drunken girls singing Britney Spears at 1AM on a Wednesday. It's not my dream neighborhood, that's for sure. But I'd just spent some time getting intimate with my house. Getting to know her in her darkness. I'd just spent some time hunkered down inside her walls, and what's more than that, I'd just spent some time with my neighbors, sharing in the same unfortunate circumstance. We watched a fire, shared some gasoline water, groaned and laughed, sweated, cheered, and danced. And there's something to be said for that. There was something to be said for this house, which suddenly felt like my home. *My* home. Not a home I'd shared with the man I'd loved. No part of it was his anymore. And these had never been his neighbors. But they were mine. For better or for worse. Shared driveways, barbecues, cookies, lawn mowings, text messaging each other when ten cop cars converged on the block and policemen went door-to-door—all of us peeking out from behind our blinds wondering whether Jason Voorhees was loose on our street, expecting to find an abandoned hockey mask and chainsaw in the bushes the next morning. Then there were the watchdogs of the block, the Ms. Cravitzes, or the woman everyone knows will tow you if your car so much as sneaks its nose across her driveway. Crazy people and all. All mine.

I think, in that moment, coming out of that shower, stretching out on the couch in the blessed cool of my living room, I stopped fighting so much. I stopped railing against the injustice of it all.

The thing I hadn't wanted to do all along was to leave James. I loved him more than I'd ever loved anyone—in a way that I know I will never love anyone ever again—and all the years we were together, I grew crazy from it. I grew insecure. I grew uncertain. I grew into a shadow, tiptoeing in my attempts to please him. All that loving and all that doubting. All that loving and desperation to feel that same love returned. Desperation doesn't look good on anyone. The tension stored up in my body over the years. My power drained to half, and then finally, there was none. I was reduced to cowering on the floor, in the dark—metaphorically speaking. It always felt like he had all the control, that I was a victim to my love for him.

Victim. And that is precisely when it stops being authentic love.

Loving someone is never a weakness. I thought I loved him even while I was saying that we couldn't be together—thought I was deeply *in love* with him. But when I said the words, I was finally deeply loving *me*. I was bleeding to death inside from all the cuts I'd received over the years, and I knew I had to stage a rescue. How could I love him without also loving me? How could I possibly be honoring him if I wasn't honoring myself? It just doesn't work that way. We have to love ourselves. We have to embrace ourselves. We must be true to ourselves before we can be true to someone else. The second I stopped being true to myself was the moment I began to do us *both* a disservice.

Perhaps I was loving him more than ever by letting him go, and I was loving myself more than ever by letting him go. I was freeing us both. It was the hardest thing I'd ever done, opening my hand like that. Walking away like that. Being willing to sit with the worst pain I've ever felt, and to STAY with it. Not to run away, not to bury it in something else, but to see it through. To allow everything around me to crumble into dust, and then to see if I could build a life from it. And I could. In time, new things formed. New life grew from seeds I worked hard to plant.

Did I make the right choice? If I had it to do again, would I have walked away from him from the start? In the end, would I have chosen to stay?

I would not have traded my time with him for the world, even if I could have saved myself all of this aftermath. My relationship with him allowed me to experience what it was like to care for someone so much and still find the courage to walk away when it became necessary to do so—when my authentic self reared up and *demanded* that I move toward the path that would put me back to work on the Project that is my Self.

When we're in service to life, I feel we have a responsibility to grow as human beings—even if that means making difficult choices that require every ounce of our courage to enact. I believe we always know the path that is going to enhance our growth…if we quiet ourselves enough to listen to our hearts, if we're brave enough to be alone for long enough to listen. James and I reached a point where, together, we were no longer our best selves. That wasn't what I wanted for either of us.

The beautiful thing about this experience, for you and for me, is that there is no right or wrong answer. It might feel like a test, but if so, please realize that no matter what answer you put down, **YOU PASS**. That's all there is to it. When you're ready to be somewhere else, then you'll put one foot in front of the other and move. It's just life. Beautiful. Amazing. Painful. Joyful. Loving is in every facet, every tear, every smile, every time you curl up in a ball wanting to disappear, every time you are hurt to the very depths of your being…love.

I always had the power to change things—my very own bucket truck and hard hat. I was never, ever as weak as I thought. And nothing about my life, in this moment, spoke of weakness. I had chosen to stay—in this city, in this house. At the start, I had no friends. I had no life aside from my job. And these things were entirely my own fault. They had never been his. So I worked to change it. In under a year, I *had* changed it. The testament to it was everywhere. I was part of a writing community, finally. I had peers I greatly respected, friends who knew me and loved me. There were people I could call if I were in need. I belonged to something important, and I was forming partnerships that were furthering my growth in ways my partnership with James simply could not do.

All those things I had wanted before, to share my work, to be inspired…I HAD those things. Maybe not in the form I'd been imagining, but in *some* form. I am sharing my life. I can call up a friend when I am feeling down. I can ask for a hug. I can help others with their own work. I am gaining encouragement in my own creative pursuits. I can offer love to a friend who needs love because I have love to spare.

It isn't a soulmate. It isn't the man of my dreams adoring me. It isn't all of my fairy tale wishes coming true (and the happily-ever-after is always a work-in-progress). Instead, it is me being ME, without the shame and anxiety and off-balance madness I felt when I was in a relationship. It is me, free of the exhaustion that comes with trying, constantly, to figure out how to *get* love. It is the fullness of me, *all* of me, surrendering to whatever comes next.

Power Restored.

ACKNOWLEDGEMENTS

I DID NOT take this journey alone. I would like to thank my family for their love and support during one of the most difficult periods of my life—with a special thanks to my mother, who endured every rumination, examination, and more than a few full-blown tearful tirades railing against the injustice of just about *everything*.

To Barbara J. Welch: You are an extraordinary woman whose words have picked me up off the floor more times than I can count; who has always had my heart in mind; and whose wisdom, humor, and general awesomeness have served as an inspiration. BJ, your friendship is an invaluable blessing in my life. Truly, you have helped me to grow.

To Scott Woods: Poet extraordinaire, host and co-founder of the Writers' Block Poetry Night, author of *We Over Here Now*, and my ambassador of irreverence. Scott, you made me laugh when I thought no one could. You welcomed me into your community, and it's an honor to call you my friend.

To the post-show Writers' Block crew: Our Wednesday nights make every other day better.

To the real-life "James": This book would not have been possible without the journey you and I took together. *Thank you for everything; I have no complaint whatsoever.*

Last, but not least, to the man of my dreams: Perhaps life is conspiring, quite remarkably, to bring us together.

RECOMMENDED READING

Susan Piver, *The Wisdom of a Broken Heart* (Free Press)

Charlotte Joko Beck, *Everyday Zen* (Harper One)

Pema Chödrön, *Comfortable with Uncertainty*
(Shambhala Publications)

Pema Chödrön, *When Things Fall Apart* (Shambhala Publications)

John M. Ortiz, Ph.D., *The Tao of Music: Using Music to
Change Your Life* (Red Wheel/Weiser)

Byron Katie, *A Thousand Names for Joy: Living in Harmony with the
Way Things Are* (Harmony)

David Richo, *The Five Things We Cannot Change and the Happiness
We Find by Embracing Them* (Shambhala Publications)

David Richo, *How to be An Adult in Relationships: The Five Keys to
Mindful Loving* (Shambhala Publications)

Don Miguel Ruiz, *The Mastery of Love: A Practical Guide to the Art
of Relationship* (Amber-Allen Publishing)

Shel Silverstein, *The Missing Piece Meets the Big O* (Harper & Row)

Judy Ford, *Single: The Art of Being Satisfied, Fulfilled and
Independent* (Adams Media)

ENDNOTES

1 Nicholas Wade, *Your Body Is Younger Than You Think*, http://www.nytimes.com/2005/08/02/science/02cell.html?pagewanted=all (May 2012)

2 Wikipedia, *Trimurti*, http://en.wikipedia.org/wiki/Trimurti#cite_note-20 (June 2012)

3 Neurogistics, Inc., The Brain Wellness Program, *What Are Neurotransmitters,* http://www.neurogistics.com/TheScience/WhatareNeurotransmi09CE.asp (May 2012)

4 American Psychological Society, *Journal of Neurophysiology*, "Reward, Addiction, and Emotion Regulation Systems Associated with Rejection in Love," http://jn.physiology.org/content/104/1/51.full (May 2012)

5 *Ibid.*

6 Tamera Cohen, *Nursing a Broken Heart? How Taking a Paracetamol Could Dull the Pain of Rejection*, http://www.dailymail.co.uk/health/article-2105813/The-pill-mend-broken-heart-Scientists-claim-simple-painkillers-dull-pain-rejection.html_(May 2012)

7 Wikipedia, *Traditional Chinese Medicine*, http://en.wikipedia.org/wiki/Accupressure#Acupuncture_and_moxibustion (July 2012)

8 Wikipedia, *Meditation*, http://en.wikipedia.org/wiki/Meditation (July 2012)

9 Brain Research Bulletin, Catherine E. Kerr, Stephanie R. Jones, Qiam Wan, Dominique L. Pritchett, Rachel H. Wasserman, Anna Wexler, Joel J. Villanueva, Jessica R. Shaw, Sara W. Lazar, Ted J. Kaptchuk, Ronnie Littenberg, Matti S. Hamalainen, Christopher I Moore, "Effects of mindfulness meditation training on anticipatory alpha modulation in primary somatosensory cortex," http://dx.doi.org/10.1016/j.brainresbull.2011.03.026 (July 2012)

10 *Science News*, (orig. author) Mark Wheeler, *Meditation Reduces Loneliness*, http://www.sciencedaily.com/releases/2012/08/120814213630.htm?utm_source=feedburner&utm_medium=feed&utm_campaign=Feed%3A+sciencedaily%2Fmind_brain%2Fspirituality+%28ScienceDaily%3A+Mind+&+Brain+News+--+Spirituality%29&utm_content=Google+Reader (August 2012)

11 Wikipedia, *Biomusicology*, http://en.wikipedia.org/wiki/Biomusicological (August 2012)

12 Wikipedia, *Entrainment (biomusicology)*, http://en.wikipedia.org/wiki/
    Entrainment_%28biomusicology%29 (August 2012)

13 Rick Groleau (NOVA), *Resonance in Strings*, http://www.pbs.org/wgbh/
    nova/elegant/resonance.html (June 2012)

14 Wikipedia, *String Theory*, http://en.wikipedia.org/wiki/String_theory
    (June 2012)

15 *Ibid.*

16 Ernest Becker, *The Denial of Death* (New York, NY: Free Press Paperbacks,
    1973)

17 *Ibid.*

18 *Who Knows What's Good or Bad: A Story*, used by permission from The
    Field Project Course 2.0

19 Wikipedia, *Geshe Chekhawa*, http://en.wikipedia.org/wiki/Geshe_Chek-
    hawa (October 2012)